"There's no better place to hear God speak than through scriptural meditation, and there's no better guide for the how-tos than Jan Johnson. *Savoring God's Word* can direct you or your group toward heart-felt encounters with God."

— KLAUS ISSLER
professor of Christian Ed & Theology, author of Wasting Time with God

"Jan Johnson's book *Savoring God's Word* is a feast. Deep in its understanding of Scriptural meditation and simple in helping the reader to grasp the important practice, this book enables all to hear God's word and for God to grow us into his image."

—TOM PARKER
director, Fuller Theological Seminary Southwest

SAVORING
GOD'S
WORD

CULTIVATING THE
SOUL-TRANSFORMING PRACTICE OF
SCRIPTURE MEDITATION

SAVORING GOD'S WORD

JAN JOHNSON

NAVPRESS®

BRINGING TRUTH TO LIFE

To Connie Kappes—
big sister, good friend, loving mother.

The Navigators is an international Christian organization. Our mission is to reach, disciple, and equip people to know Christ and to make Him known through successive generations. We envision multitudes of diverse people in the United States and every other nation who have a passionate love for Christ, live a lifestyle of sharing Christ's love, and multiply spiritual laborers among those without Christ.

NavPress is the publishing ministry of The Navigators. NavPress publications help believers learn biblical truth and apply what they learn to their lives and ministries. Our mission is to stimulate spiritual formation among our readers.

© 2004 by Jan Johnson

All rights reserved. No part of this publication may be reproduced in any form without written permission from NavPress, P.O. Box 35001, Colorado Springs, CO 80935.

www.navpress.com

NAVPRESS, BRINGING TRUTH TO LIFE, and the NAVPRESS logo are registered trademarks of NavPress. Absence of ® in connection with marks of NavPress or other parties does not indicate an absence of registration of those marks.

ISBN 1-57683-399-2

Cover and interior design by David Carlson Design

Cover photo by Damir Frkovic / Masterfile

Creative Team: Terry Behimer, Traci Mullins, Amy Spencer, Darla Hightower, Glynese Northam

Some of the anecdotal illustrations in this book are true to life and are included with the permission of the persons involved. All other illustrations are composites of real situations, and any resemblance to people living or dead is coincidental.

Unless otherwise identified, all Scripture quotations in this publication are taken from the *Holy Bible: New International Version*® (NIV®). Copyright © 1973, 1978, 1984 by International Bible Society. Used by permission of Zondervan Publishing House. All rights reserved. Other versions used include *The Message: New Testament with Psalms and Proverbs* (MSG) by Eugene H. Peterson, copyright © 1993, 1994, 1995, used by permission of NavPress Publishing Group; the *New Revised Standard Version* (NRSV), copyright © 1989, by the Division of Christian Education of the National Council of the Churches of Christ in the USA, used by permission, all rights reserved; and the *King James Version* (KJV).

Johnson, Jan, 1947-
  Savoring God's word : cultivating the soul-transforming practice of
scripture meditation / Jan Johnson.
    p. cm.
Includes bibliographical references.
  ISBN 1-57683-399-2
  1. Bible--Meditations. 2. Meditation--Christianity. I. Title.
  BS4913.J64 2004
  248.3'4--dc21

                    2003012052

Printed in Canada

1 2 3 4 5 6 7 8 9 10 / 08 07 06 05 04

FOR A FREE CATALOG OF
NAVPRESS BOOKS & BIBLE STUDIES,
CALL 1-800-366-7788 (USA)
OR 1-416-499-4615 (CANADA)

CONTENTS

ACKNOWLEDGMENTS

I am grateful to M. Robert Mulholland of Asbury Seminary, whose teaching and example led me from casual Scripture meditation to regular daily adventures in *lectio divina*. I also owe a great "debt of love" to teacher and friend Dallas Willard, who continually challenges us all to consider transformation into Christlikeness.

My thanks to Terry Behimer of NavPress, who heard my passion about this book and believed in me. I'm grateful to have had both Terry and Traci Mullins walk alongside me.

As always, gratitude is due to my husband, cheerleader, and diligent proofreader, Greg Johnson. My adult children, Jeff and Janae Johnson, have been good sports in trying out exercises now and then.

INTRODUCTION

How to Use This Book

❧

Welcome to an adventure in learning to meditate on Scripture. This is a book that you read as you would read any other, but it also includes exercises throughout. It's a book you use, as well as read. As you read along and are introduced to a practice of meditation, I often lead you informally into a time of meditation on a passage of Scripture. You may feel nervous about whether you're doing the meditation exercise right, because you haven't read all the instructions in the book yet, but don't concern yourself with that. My purpose is to help you to try meditating as you read the book. You'll receive further instructions as we move along. When an exercise occurs within a chapter, pause and try it. Meditation is like everything else: you learn by doing. And I want to entice you to practice without worrying about whether you're doing it exactly right.

At the end of each chapter are questions for you to reflect on and more meditation exercises for you to try. Please don't skip them. The book will have a different and surprising effect on you if you do all the exercises. Some exercises include instructions to group leaders, which appear in boxes, but ignore them if you are not in a group.

Besides using this book as an individual, you can use it in the following ways:

Book study groups—To study the book a chapter at a time, group members will ideally read the assigned chapter before meeting, also experiencing the exercises within the chapter on their own. (There are eight chapters and seven exercises in appendix B, so eight to fifteen meetings are possible, depending on how much group meditation your group wants to do.) Together the group should read appendix A, "Guidelines for Group Meditation." These instructions explain how to do the meditations with a permanent leader or rotating leaders. The leader will want to read appendix A beforehand to be prepared for the first session.

At the group meetings based on chapters 1–8, the leader can use this as the first question each time: *What, if anything, was said in this chapter that has made you think?* If nothing made participants think, ask them to choose what most resonated with them. Urge participants to look for the answer to this question and underline it as they read the chapter.

Then discuss the questions provided at the end of each chapter and do the exercises designed for group interaction or discussion, when provided. The discussion is important because meditation may be unfamiliar and group members need to process it with others. Occasionally, additional instructions for groups are provided for certain questions.

Bible study groups—Most Bible study groups use studies with the familiar format of reading a passage and answering questions about it. These questions typically invite participants to observe what the Scripture says, to interpret it, and then to apply it. The format for these meditations is different because it provides more interaction with God.

To use this book in a Bible study meeting, group members need to read the book (at least chapters 1–5) before their first meeting. As they do so, they will experience meditation exercises within the chapters on their own and reflect on the questions at the end of the chapters. Then, as a group, they can meet each time and do one or more of the group exercises in chapters 6–8 and appendix B. For the first few meetings, the group should read together appendix A, "Guidelines for Group Meditation." The leader will want to read that beforehand to be prepared for the first session.

A *personal retreat*—This book may be used for a one-day or multi-day private retreat. Simply read through the book and do the exercises. Take breaks after exercises that are particularly riveting and allow plenty of time for journaling as needed. (Suggestions for journaling are included in chapter 4.)

A *group retreat without an outside speaker*—Churches that wish to have a retreat with a lot of interaction with God but without an outside speaker may use this book as a resource. A leader or team of leaders needs to read the book and practice the exercises beforehand. After reading the book, the leader can introduce a point or two from each chapter and then lead participants through one of the exercises. For example, a four-session retreat could be structured this way:

> Session 1: *chapters 1–5 and an exercise (choose from the ones at the end of chapters 4 or 5)*
> Session 2: *chapter 6 and the exercise at the end*
> Session 3: *chapter 7 and one of the exercises within the chapter*
> Session 4: *chapter 8 and one of the exercises at the end*

Or the leader may use an exercise from appendix B instead of one from the chapters. When leading with a team, the speaker-leader may change for each session. This communicates to participants that meditation is not a matter of personality, because they see different types of people using it.

Personal mentoring or spiritual direction—As a mentor or spiritual director, you may see that the person who wants to be discipled or directed needs to grow in a certain direction that the exercises in appendix B deal with: finding intimacy with God, healing life's wounds, having the heart of Christ, building relationships, and making progress in the spiritual life. If so, you can do the exercise during a session together or suggest that the one being mentored or directed do it between sessions.

As you start using this book in some form, ask God to speak to you. Hearing from God will transform your soul.

Chapter One

WHY MEDITATE?

A PATH TO SPIRITUAL TRANSFORMATION

As I walked through the church parking lot to my car, I wanted to scream. I could hear the voices of two couples discussing an upcoming vote within the church, and they were attacking those who disagreed with them. How could they do this? They had just participated in a class where we had seen from Scripture that the most important issue is whether people love each other. I'd even commented that our choice to love each other was more crucial than the outcome of the vote. I'd challenged them, asking, "Would we behave like disciples of Jesus in the midst of disagreement? Would we speak the truth in love? Would we listen and be present to each other or would we pigeonhole people, call each other names, and look for ways to manipulate the undecided?"

I tried not to listen, but now they'd begun skewering a certain person and grilling her until charred. I got in my car, laid my head on the steering wheel, and wept. Why is it that we know the facts of Scripture so well but do not put them into practice?

But as I drove home I thought, *Why am I surprised?* After all, I was asking them to look within their hearts. That's difficult work. A class discussion about love does not transform us into people who love. At first I had felt as agitated as they were. But when I asked God how I should vote and meditated on Scripture, I sensed God coaxing me: *Don't forget to love.* I realized that I needed to listen and love rather than insist everyone look at it my way. I needed to discuss the issue without being rude or irritated (see 1 Corinthians 13:5). This situation was testing me as a person and giving me an opportunity to taste and see what it's like to love people when I disagree with them. My change of heart and behavior occurred because I'd heard from God myself. That's what transforms people—not being told what to do.

Besides, the gap between what we say and how we behave is enormous. I say I believe in telling the truth, but I exaggerate to impress someone. I say I have faith in God, but my confidence in God is shaken when people fail and I try to rescue them.

These faithless behaviors flow from stubborn habits and ingrained character flaws that we can't seem to get rid of. Many Christians lament that they can't overcome tendencies to criticize, complain, and procrastinate. For myself, my common flaws are grouchiness and laziness.

The stubbornness of these entrenched attitudes makes us wonder how God changes people at all. We tell new Christians that the Holy Spirit will change them, but we don't say how. They become discouraged when they don't see it happen.

As a result, I've spent years trying to discover how God changes people. I'm haunted by the man James described, who looked in the mirror, walked away, and forgot what he looked like (see James 1:22-25). In the midst of sermons, Bible studies, and others' pointed comments, we look in the mirrors of our lives and see valleys of failures. We promise God we'll change, but so often we don't.

We think we'll change if we're taught better, so we look for the best teachers. I've spent twenty years writing adult Bible study sessions, specializing in insightful application activities. I've prayed that the teachers using the materials I've written will never be the same after preparing the lesson and that their students will see it and be changed too. But I'm also an avid churchgoer, the wife of someone who has been a pastor. I know the dull truth: Many of us use God to gain a better life, but our character changes very little. I've watched new Christians encounter God in a deep way only to graduate to a life of nonstop church activity. All that activity can become a substitute for a life lived in union with God. When people do not arrange their life around cultivating their interior life with God, they tend to become only vaguely nicer versions of who they used to be.

It's true that those who participate in Bible studies may begin to form an interactive life with God, but too often they switch the focus to correctly filling out the answers to the study questions, participating well in discussion, or listening to others' inspiring stories. None of those things are wrong—they're just not the point: knowing God. Or Christians read through the Bible in a year, which can be helpful; but if they do it to fulfill a daily obligation instead of to interact with God, they miss the point. Each day that they find themselves caught up with the reading schedule, they feel good about their Christian life. After all, they're achieving something! If you ask them if the reading is nourishing their inner life with God and transforming their soul, they're not sure how to respond. When based on achievement, even these beneficial activities do not nourish a relationship with God. Instead, they tend to create a self-satisfied sense of having accomplished something "spiritual."

This lack of intimate connection with God in the midst of spiritual activity explains the entrenchment of our Christless habits. When our interior life with God languishes, we will not be transformed. Instead, we can only *try to be good.* But as unregenerate human beings, we don't naturally long to be the kinds of people described in Jesus'

Sermon on the Mount: those who have a heart for their enemies, who speak simply instead of defending themselves, who gladly go the extra mile instead of complaining about the person who dares to ask.

WHAT DOES SEEKING GOD LOOK LIKE?

Try this question on the ordinary people who attend your church or small group: How are you seeking God?

Does this question baffle them or do their faces light up as they explain the latest exchange in their rich relationship with God? The point of our discipleship is "to know Christ and the power of the resurrection," but few of us know how to help that happen. We know we need to seek God, but do we know what seeking God looks like in the life of someone with our temperament and daily routines?

If we were to offer these ordinary folks some ideas for how to seek God, what would we give them as patterns? From the Scripture itself and from the experiences of those who have sought God throughout the ages, we have heard about spiritual disciplines or exercises or strategies—whatever we wish to call them. As we put them into place in our lives, they help us connect with God day in and day out. For example, we *pray* in ways that connect us with God in all of life, because we have experimented with what works and does not work for us. We *interact with Scripture* in ways that help us know God, not simply know about God. We *serve* with a conscious awareness of God's presence so our service is permeated with back-and-forth communication with God.

Such exercises or strategies focus us on God in all of life. Then when calamities and chaos smack us front and center, we are not derailed. Instead we seek God through these disciplines we are so familiar with. We may wobble, but we are so centered in God that we're less likely to fall into despair and to harm others with our discouragement, disgust, or anger.

These disciplines or exercises help us connect with God so the Holy Spirit can work within us to transform our souls. They are not advanced options just for the "elite" Christian; they are essential paths for us to live in intimate union with God while breathing on this planet.

Scripture meditation as a spiritual discipline is soul-transforming. As we sit in Scripture and ponder it (instead of skimming over it or limiting our interaction with it to study), all parts of ourselves are fascinated by the ways and doings of God. We begin to long for more of God in our life. As C. S. Lewis wrote, we experience "the scent of a flower we have not found, the echo of a tune we have not heard, news from a country we have never yet visited."[1] God implants in us a desire for a far-off country, which is God's own self.

The more we experience God this way, the more eagerly we carve out moments of solitude with God. This interaction with God affects us so deeply in our core that we become much more likely to respond to people with a quiet presence, a readiness to listen, and a desire to love them. When we connect with God through such strategies, the gap between our belief and our behavior shrinks. We obey in a more natural, automatic way because our hearts have been transformed.

For example, in a meeting with my spiritual director, I mentioned something I'd done that was unusually wise and obedient for me. I'd found myself in a slippery place of temptation and without thinking I turned away from it even though it made me appear less congenial. Not until later did I realize I had steered myself out of the way of temptation. I looked at my spiritual director in bewilderment and said, "How did I do that? Whatever I did, I need to keep doing it!" His question answered my question: "What have you been meditating on?" I laughed. I'd been living in the words and phrases of the Sermon on the

Mount for about a year (see Matthew 5). My unJanlike, upright behavior had automatically reflected that passage. This is how spiritual formation works. You do the connecting with God, and God does the perfecting in you.

INTERACTING WITH GOD THROUGH MEDITATION

This book is about learning to meditate on Scripture so you can better connect with and interact with God. Although we'll explore the details, tips, and potential blunders in Scripture meditation later, for now let me say that meditating is taking time to read a passage slowly and bringing all of our mind to the passage in quiet alertness. Instead of analyzing the words, we *enter into* the passage, letting the words be spoken to us by the Holy Spirit to see what impact they will make on us. Meditation usually involves quieting oneself, reading the passage, rereading it, and then shutting our eyes to see what stands out to us today. Then we pray the Scripture so that we are dialoguing with God. God speaks to us in Scripture and we respond in prayer.

This process creates an interaction with God so that instead of merely reading words, we "taste and see that the LORD is good" (Psalm 34:8). Instead of knowing *about* God, we come to know and experience God. Such focus stores the words, ideas, and images of Scripture in our minds, feelings, and even our bodies in a way that affects our behavior later. This often-overlooked practice, when rooted in the Holy Spirit's power and direction, is one of the many long-used, Scripture-recommended tools that are essential in building a rich and life-transforming relationship with God.

Without personal strategies for connecting with God, our daily agendas tend to become: I must have . . . I must be . . . I must achieve . . . But exercises such as Scripture meditation *cultivate* the heart and guard it from those stubborn habits (see Proverbs 4:23; 23:19). Having a cultivated heart means that we become more and more inclined to look at life as Jesus did. As a result, we talk and serve and move more like Jesus. We react as Jesus did—loving people and using things instead of loving things and using people. The Holy Spirit does the cultivating as we choose to meditate on God and God's ways.

Scripture meditation can even retrain the divided heart (see Psalm 86:11). Most of the time the heart is torn between cooperating with God and getting needs met in destructive ways (or mediocre ways that substitute for seeking God). We want to humble ourselves, but we also want to show off; to submit to the other person, but also to have our own way; to respect others' choices, but also to force them to comply with ours. When living a life that involves little interaction with God, we find obedience to be a heavy burden that makes us feel weary about going to church.

But obedience doesn't have to be some unpleasant thing we have to pressure ourselves to do. When we routinely connect with God, we want to obey. Or we at least *want to want* to obey. The burden is lighter. The yoke of obedience is actually the easier way to live life.

This truth—that connecting leads to perfecting—is detailed in the text of Joshua 1:8: "Do not let this Book of the Law depart from your mouth; meditate on it day and night, *so that you may be careful to do* everything written in it. Then you will be prosperous and successful" (emphasis added). When we regularly meditate on God's laws of goodness, something changes inside us and we more naturally become "careful to do" them. We want to do them. Goodness flows instead of being forced.

As God speaks to us in our Scripture meditation, we come to love God more, which helps us see the true goodness of obedience (see John 13:34-35; 14:21). We trust God more and have more confidence in the ways of God. We believe that if we follow God, we won't have a boring life but one full of intriguing moments and unexpected adventures.

Having words, phrases, and images of Scripture dancing in our heads keeps us so connected with God that we are changed at the heart level. We actually want to be humble or love our enemy. Exercises such as meditation allow God to ravish us with the divine personality and draw us toward the kingdom life that understands that humility makes life so much easier, so free of striving, competing, and proving ourselves.

Practicing the specific skills of meditation (which I'll explain later) helps us in all of life. They teach us to have a listening heart, which opens us to God through these inner attitudes that Quaker author Douglas Steere lists:

- *Vulnerability—I can open my truest feelings, motives, and thoughts to God.*
- *Expectancy—I can expect God to meet my needs in this space of time.*
- *Acceptance—I can accept whatever happens in this quiet time.*
- *Constancy—(the Latin and Greek word meaning to "stand with" or to "stay with"): I can rely on God to stand with me, to keep watch on my soul, not to get fed up with me.*[2]

Meditation retrains our mind to have the mind of Christ. For example, while practicing *lectio divina* (pronounced *LEX-ee-oh dih-VEE-nuh*[3]; method of Scripture meditation described in chapter 6), I was surprised that God told Ezekiel to "look closely and listen attentively and set your mind upon all that I shall show you" (Ezekiel 40:4, NRSV). As I read, I wondered why God would give such elementary instruction to someone as faithful as Ezekiel (as I'd noted in the previous thirty-nine chapters). Yet God thought it was important to command this devoted prophet never to waver from paying attention and listening. If Ezekiel needed to hear these words, I certainly did too.

Pondering this fresh insight, I prayed and asked God what it would look like today for me to look closely, listen attentively, and set my mind on God's words and actions. I waited in silence. What came to me (I believe through the Holy Spirit) involved a posture or way of being I needed to cultivate: listening fully to the people around me—eyes wide and mouth closed—instead of thinking of what I would say next. In conversations I needed to ask God to show me how to be Jesus in these other persons' lives rather than saying whatever came into my head. This is what I'd seen Jesus do in the Gospels. He was not a hit-and-run teacher or healer, but someone who was fully present to people—looking and listening and loving those with whom he interacted (see Matthew 19:26; Mark 10:21; Luke 2:46; 20:17; John 1:42).

After such times of meditation, God's phrases resonate in you. Your behavior is supernaturally transformed because it flows out of the mind of Christ.

Training, Not Trying

Connecting with God through spiritual disciplines (or exercises or strategies) is different from trying to be good. I remember how I used to read 1 Corinthians 13:4-8 and beat myself up. Was I patient? No. Was I kind? No. Did I envy? Yes. I failed the test nearly every time.

While meditating on the passage, it occurred to me that because God is love, the descriptions of love were also descriptions of God. Because God is love, God is then patient and kind. God does not envy or boast. God is not proud or rude or self-seeking or easily irritated. God doesn't keep a record of wrongs. God doesn't delight in evil, but rejoices in truth. No matter what, God always protects, always trusts, always hopes, always perseveres. God never fails.

As I tasted these words over and over, I felt so grateful that God doesn't keep a record of *my* wrongs, that God isn't rude to *me,* no matter how discourteously or braggadociosly I behave. I felt such love for this God who always protects, always trusts, always hopes, always perseveres. I am often cynical, but God always hopes. I am suspicious, but God always trusts. I sensed my outlook shifting. After meditating on this passage one day (I was so familiar with it by this time I could meditate on it as I hiked), I decided not to *have a talk* with my then twenty-one-year-old son about a rude remark he'd made. Instead I would continue to love and encourage him. I followed through, and a few days later, the opportunity arose to mention—lightly and casually—the more desirable behavior. He smiled and said, "Oh. Okay." How different our interchange was because I was so intrigued by God's personality of love.

If you will, go back over the second paragraph in this section that begins with, "While meditating on the passage . . ." Read it a few times. Sit in these ideas. Shut your eyes. What is God saying to you today?[4] Don't worry at this point about whether you're doing this right. Just try it out.

Questions and Activities for Individual Reflection or Group Discussion

If you're reading this book on your own, go over these questions to turn the ideas of the chapter over in your mind. If you're part of a group reading the book, use these questions to discuss the ideas. Listen carefully to learn what you can from the insights of others.

1.   What, if anything, was said in this chapter that has made you think?

2.   What idea or phrase most resonates with you or agrees with what you believe God has been saying to you lately?

3.   It's been said that many Christians have substituted the busyness of

outward church activities for an inward life with God. Why do you think that happens?

4. Turn to 1 Corinthians 13:4-8. Close your eyes and ask the Holy Spirit to speak to you. Then read the passage aloud and sit quietly for a while. What do you believe God is saying to you that you need to hear?

Group leader instructions for question 4: After a group member reads the passage aloud and the group waits in silence, members open their eyes and take turns *briefly* reporting what they believe God said to them. They should be careful not to interrupt each other or evaluate what others say. Just listen to and pray for the person speaking.

Chapter Two

WHY PEOPLE DON'T MEDITATE

COMMON REASONS FOR RESISTANCE

✿

In spite of the rich benefits and long practice of meditation, this discipline confounds and turns off some disciples of Jesus. They think, *Meditation must be some new and trendy thing—let's stick to plain old Bible study. Meditation sounds too mystical. Isn't it something only monks do? It's probably too hard for someone like me to practice as a spiritual discipline. Besides, don't New Age folks do this? Doesn't that make it wrong?*

Let's look at these protests that meditation might not be a true, good, or readily accessible way to connect with God.

UNFAMILIAR TERRITORY

To the early hearers in Scripture, meditation apparently was not unfamiliar territory but a natural and welcome spiritual practice. Otherwise the Psalms would not mention meditation so often—sixteen times in the New International Version.[1] The psalmist meditated all day long on the law, finding intriguing thoughts that led to genuine goodness instead of to the phoniness of being goody-goody. Meditating on Scripture gave the psalmists wisdom that surpassed that of their teachers and enemies, led to diligent obedience, and kept them out of temptation's way. And it wasn't a miserable process—God's words tasted sweeter than honey (see Psalm 119:97-101,103).

Scripture itself gives us specific instructions to pause, to reflect, and to listen to God. Seventy-one times in Psalms and three times in Habakkuk, the musical notation *Selah* reminds the reader to stop and reflect. A number of scholars agree that *Selah* was inserted at those points where the reader or singer should pause to reflect "in order that the statement last made or the thought as a whole just developed may be reflected upon before the next turn of the thought appears."[2] Through these *Selah* reminders, God shows us the importance of pausing in our thought processes to ponder truth.

Still, Scripture doesn't tell us *how* to meditate. That's because Middle Easterners in Old and New Testament times knew how to meditate, just as they knew how to fast. As a result, no instructions for fasting or meditation are given. But we can talk to others who are practiced in fasting and meditation to find out how to approach these exercises.

Perhaps meditation also is not carefully explained in Scripture because there are so many ways to do it. Just as there is no single right way to study the Bible or pray, many methods of meditation exist. So we approach these various ways experimentally to see what is most helpful. We start with something simple and innovate as needed.

Meditation probably is not as unfamiliar to contemporary Christians as they may think. If you've enjoyed biblical word studies or word pictures, you've dabbled in Scripture meditation. For example, you can use your imagination to meditate on the idea in Isaiah 26:3 of being "stayed": "Thou wilt keep him in perfect peace, whose mind is stayed on thee: because he trusteth in thee" (KJV). The original Hebrew word for "stayed" is a word used to describe the way a rope is fastened to a tent peg. Imagine powerful Middle Eastern winds pulling on the ropes that fastened down the enormous tents that Israelite herdsman lived in. Their clothes may have flapped furiously in the wind, but the tent peg (and therefore the tent) stayed in place because of the powerful tension on that rope. In the same way, when we experience tornado-like chaos in our lives, our goal is to keep our minds *stayed* on God.

Isn't This an Eastern Practice?

When many folks hear the word *meditation,* they think of the deceased Beatles musician George Harrison. Or they think of a Buddhist monk sitting in a pretzel position chanting "Ohhmmmm . . . " If Buddhists and Hindus meditate, should Christians also do it? Implied in this protest is that Christians should not use any spiritual discipline used by other world religions. Does that logic work? Even though the Bible urges us to pray, Hindu leader Mahatma Gandhi prayed. Are we banned from praying? Even though the apostles quoted Jesus, so does the Dalai Lama, the leader of Tibetan Buddhism. Must we stop quoting Jesus? We're left with this decision: Should we do the things Jesus did and the positive practices mentioned in the Bible, or should we refrain from anything another world religion does?

The issue is not the method but the goal. Consider that in Eastern religions, meditation is generally a matter of coming to a place of nothingness. In Christianity, meditation is about entering into a text of Scripture. When we meditate on a Gospel, it's a meeting with Jesus.

IT'S NEW AND TRENDY

Closely linked to the objection that meditation is practiced by Eastern religions is that it's something New Age people have made popular. The truth is that meditation is not new and trendy but old and classic.

What makes Christian meditation classic is its roots in ancient Judeo-Christian practice. For example, the Old Testament practice of celebrating the Passover involved the Hebrews and later the Jews reenacting their last meal before fleeing Egypt, eating in preparation for the exodus journey. They even copied what the original Hebrews wore and ate and how they ate (see Exodus 12:11; Numbers 9:2-3).

In chapter 7 we'll examine the Ignatian method of Scripture meditation, which is also about reliving a biblical event. Those who follow this method "strive to participate in the actual event by projecting themselves back into the historical happening to try to become a part of the scene in order to draw some practical fruit for their life."[3]

Another method of meditation, *lectio divina,* was developed by the fourth century, and probably before that.[4] Lectio is rooted in the wisdom literature practices of "laying hold" and "keeping": "When I was a boy in my father's house, still tender, and an only child of my mother, he taught me and said, '*Lay hold* of my words with all your heart; *keep* my commands and you will live'" (Proverbs 4:3-4, emphasis added). To "lay hold" or to "keep" a Scripture passage is to listen with the ear of our heart, not just to take in information. *Lay hold* and *keep* "are terms that invite us to ponder, to reflect, to turn something over and over until it becomes part of our being."[5]

In the New Testament we see how reflective Mary stored up in her heart, pondered, and treasured events that would be written of in our Gospels (see Luke 2:19,51). The word that describes Mary's treasuring of Jesus' words after he had stayed behind in Jerusalem at age twelve is a Greek word meaning "to keep" (*diatereo*). "To keep carefully" describes how you store treasures in a scrapbook and pore over them for years to come. (Mary's example also reminds us that meditation is not just for the spiritually elite. This teenage girl probably couldn't even read, but she could meditate.)

Only Monks Meditate

Christians through the ages have meditated with great benefit to themselves. By the early sixth century, *lectio divina* was so familiar that monastery founder Benedict of Nursia didn't need to describe it in his guidelines for monks but simply stated that they should do it. *Lectio*—as it's usually called—was used in training monks, and Ignatius of Loyola (for whom the Ignatian method is named) founded a religious order, so some Protestants may wonder if they should be emulating such card-carrying Roman Catholics. Yet we use many spiritual tools used by Christians who came before us. A popular method of praying, the ACTS acronym (adoration, confession, thanksgiving, and supplication), has its roots in Catholic tradition.[6]

Lectio divina continued to be a primary way for Christians to connect with God until the Protestant Reformation in the early 1500s, when the Reformers discarded many practices linked to the past. Yet in the 1700s John Wesley wrote about the meditative practice of recollection: "Be sure to read, not cursorily or hastily, but leisurely, seriously, and with great attention; with proper pauses and intervals, and that you may allow time for the enlightenings of the divine grace."[7]

Twentieth-century scholar Dietrich Bonhoeffer, who taught at an underground seminary in Germany during World War II, included meditation as a regular part of the students' training. "In meditation God's Word seeks to enter in and remain with us," he wrote. "It strives to stir us, to work and operate in us, so that we shall not get away from it the whole day long. Then it will do its work in us, often without our being conscious of it."[8]

IT'S TOO MYSTICAL

Because meditation is open-ended instead of precise, it may be more mystical than Christians steeped in modernity are used to. The views of modernity that have permeated society and culture for the past five hundred years have largely been about conquest and control, in which a new world was discovered and two continents were conquered. Not only were there wars and revolutions, but the whole world waged war twice. Science and technology have tried to conquer disease, aging, and mildew. Through the development of the machine, we found the best, quickest ways to get things done. We treasure efficiency. Because this has been an age of analysis, we've learned to dissect things, examine them, and analyze them endlessly. All this progress has created an infatuation with newness, so that we routinely throw off old ideas, thinking that newer ones are usually better. Such "progress" also makes us extremely objective, so that, according to Brian McLaren, we replace "mysteries with comprehension, ignorance with information."[9]

While many features of modernity have helped us, they have also invaded and shaded the biblical view of faith. Such biblical exercises as meditation have too often been overlooked. Methods of meditation are not new but ancient. Surely, we think, methods of meditation that originated in premodern times can be of little use to us now. If meditation were invented yesterday and popularized in a best-selling book, it would probably have more credibility with many Christians today.

Consider that the opposite may be true. Doesn't credibility come from surviving the tests of time, from standing on the shoulders of spiritual giants? I would not write this book if I were putting forth methods I had invented or ones only I had used. I am not that wise. I look to my older brothers and sisters in the faith who have come before me. Over hundreds of years, people have tested the disciplines and found these methods credible and helpful. Many books on prayer have come and gone, but those I refer to are still in print after hundreds of years.

In the glow of modernity, spirituality is infused with notions of conquering and efficiency. It's easy to look for the most orderly, quick way to "master" a Bible text. We find ourselves praying in order to get results, forgetting that prayer is really about getting more of God within ourselves. We tend to search for machine-like ways to make our "time with God" productive. But wait—a new book has come out with a better method! The mysteries of God are solved in apologetics books. The subjective parts of Scripture—the poetry and imagery of the prophets—are less easily charted and so we don't read them as much. The products of meditation (hearing God, transformation into Christlikeness) are not precise and therefore are difficult to grade ourselves on. Simply letting the text speak is not *quick*. It involves waiting, an honored activity in Scripture, but it is generally shunned by us productive moderns. Yet Scripture recommends it, and to be a disciple of Jesus is to move beyond one's cultural bias and embrace mystery when God prescribes it.

God allowed much of Scripture to be written in poetic, mysterious terms. Even the plain text of Paul's epistles includes paradox. Consider this phrase from one of Paul's prayers: "to know this love that surpasses knowledge" (Ephesians 3:19). If this love surpasses knowledge, it cannot be known. So why bother "knowing" unknowable love? Yet grasping this unfathomable love of God is the main point of the prayer.

Also, much of Scripture's meaning is layered. What does it mean for Christ to dwell in your heart by faith (see Ephesians 3:17)? Does it mean to decide to follow Jesus? Maybe, but as you sit in this prayer day after day, you realize that even as a long-time Christian you have barely let Christ dwell in your heart at all. In time (not quickly) God shows you how much more Christlike you could look—one who has compassion on the have-nots and speaks up for justice—and so you invite Christ to dwell in you even more. You're not sure what this would look like, so you ask God to reveal it to you as you sit in it and ponder and beg God "to put into [your heart] whatever is most pleasing to him."[10]

Here is the Ephesians 3:16-21 prayer printed out in full. Which phrase in this prayer draws you to want to ponder it?

> *I pray that out of his glorious riches he may strengthen you with power through his Spirit in your inner being, so that Christ may dwell in your hearts through faith. And I pray that you, being rooted and established in love, may have power, together with all the saints, to grasp how wide and long and high and deep is the love of Christ, and to know this love that surpasses knowledge—that you may be filled to the measure of all the fullness of God. Now to him who is able to do immeasurably more than all we ask or imagine, according to his power that is at work within us, to him be glory in the church and in Christ Jesus throughout all generations, for ever and ever! Amen.*

Why did that certain phrase stand out to you? How does it connect with other things you've been hearing from God?

These are the kinds of questions we ask in meditation. Asking such questions uses "muscles" most of us moderns have not developed. We haven't trained ourselves to wait and ponder. This requires a retraining of our minds.

The truth is, Christianity itself is mystical. It insists that a divine God comes to dwell within individual disciples of Jesus and did dwell in the body of Jesus on earth (see John 14:17; Colossians 1:19). If Christianity is not mystical, how do you explain "the mystery that has been kept hidden for ages and generations" that "Christ in you" is the "hope of glory" (Colossians 1:26-27)? How do you explain that Jesus abides in believers and they have the opportunity to abide in Christ every moment (see John 15:1-8)? You cannot prove any of the previous scriptural statements in a scientific laboratory, but many Christians believe them anyway. And many have experienced them.

Meditation helps to ground the mystical facet of Christianity in an experience of Scripture. According to Dallas Willard, "Everything in principle has been said in the Bible. [In meditation], we won't have some reversal of basic doctrine. But you can't constitute a growing relationship with God on the basis of basic doctrine—the issue in meditation is personal relationship. Disciplines provide personal space in which relationship is worked out. That's where the seeking comes in—they're only for people who are seeking God."[11]

For those who understand that Christianity entails a relationship with God, meditation is important. A relationship means two beings are interacting. Scripture meditation is a relating skill, but many people prefer a cut-and-dried method of studying and praying with checklists. Building a relationship is exploring the parts of a person you're drawn to—and then the parts you're not drawn to. So is meditation.

It Sounds Too Hard!

So let's say you agree that meditation is worth trying, but you say it would be too difficult because you don't "live in your head." Meditation sounds like strenuous mental work. You feel you have no intuition, no imagination—you're an active doer. You work as a landscaper or truck driver. Consider that the most meditative person in Scripture—David, the psalm writer—was a Rambolike warrior. This ultimate doer was also a ponderer. Consider also that gardening and driving are excellent venues for pondering, once the skill is learned.

Or perhaps you're an extrovert. You love relating to people. The idea of lingering and pondering over words in quiet and solitude sounds boring. If you have such reservations, don't ignore them, but don't let them dictate what you experiment with either. Make note of them and see what happens. Being alone with God is not lonely, but it does require aloneness. Yet meditation is frequently done in groups so that the aloneness is shared in community and followed by brief reflections. (See appendix A for information on group meditation.)

Some are put off by having to learn how to do a spiritual exercise. Yet we work hard to learn to serve a volleyball well or cook a soufflé. We set aside time to lift weights or practice playing the piano. We focus our efforts on cultivating a marriage or deepening a friendship. Why then would we expect insights from God to light upon us from nowhere? To the contrary, to become a friend of the One who is incomprehensible to our finite human understanding is an adventure. It takes effort, which may seem too demanding in a passive culture in which we want things done to us and for us—entertain me, cater to my wishes, serve me fast food that tastes great.

Connecting with God in the doing of spiritual disciplines resembles digging for treasure. The treasures are God and the kingdom of God, but they are not readily noticed. Like the treasure Jesus described in Matthew 13:44, they are "hidden in a field." Jesus pictured this treasure digger as someone full of energy and determination who searched for treasure until he found it. Breathless, he buried it again in victory before anyone else saw it. Then with a grin on his face, he sold off everything he owned so he could buy that entire field. How he must have loved living in that field and enjoying his treasure.

In the same way, you decide you want to seek God. You spend your time, energy, and resources seeking God. Each time you sight glimmers of God, you grin with delight. It requires everything you have, but you learn that you never lack a thing.

Imagine yourself as this treasure digger. How does it feel to find the buried treasure you've longed for? Does it hurt all that much to sell off everything else? What do you say to yourself when you return to the field and unearth the treasure?

Don't let inner resistance deter you from what you need to do to seek God. In the spring and summer, my favorite hiking trail is full of snakes, including rattlesnakes. So I hike early in the morning before the heat of the sun draws them out. If I have to walk in the afternoon instead, I take a broader gravel road where snakes don't venture. I listen to the cautions, but I haven't stopped hiking. Why? These trails are one of my best places to pray Scripture, to hear God, to sing old hymns at the top of my voice, and to find my soul renewed. If I let snakes deter me from these hikes, I would be a much angrier, more anxious person. So I find ways around my natural resistance. That is what it means to seek God.

Questions and Activities for Individual Reflection or Group Discussion

1. What, if anything, was said in this chapter that has made you think?

2. Contemporary Christians often say that Christianity is a relationship, not a religion. If so, why are we sometimes reticent to seek personal interaction with God?

3. Read the Wesley quotation below. Which words speak to you most about the way you need to read Scripture?

> Be sure to read, not cursorily or hastily, but leisurely, seriously, and
> with great attention; with proper pauses and intervals, and that you

may allow time for the enlightenings of the divine grace. To this end, recollect, every now and then, what you have read, and consider how to reduce it to practice. . . . Read those passages over and over that more nearly concern yourself, and more closely affect your inclinations or practice.[12]

4. Ponder this verse again: "Thou wilt keep him in perfect peace, whose mind is stayed on thee: because he trusteth in thee" (Isaiah 26:3, KJV). What "winds" in life are blowing you so hard that your "tent peg" feels like it's about to be torn from the ground? Read the verse again to yourself or aloud. Shut your eyes and imagine a sturdy rope fastening you to the heart of God while the furious wind blows around you. What would you want to say to God in response?

Group leader instructions for question 4: After a group member reads aloud Isaiah 26:3 and participants wait in silence, members should open their eyes and take turns *briefly* answering the first question in number 4. Then have the verse read aloud again and wait. Group members then answer the second question. Close in prayer, asking God to help the group hear God as they learn to meditate.

Chapter Three

WHAT IS SCRIPTURE MEDITATION?

HOW MEDITATION DIFFERS FROM BIBLE STUDY

What does it take to get good grades in school? Knowing answers, retaining facts, taking tests without "choking." Most of us spent years in school learning to gather facts. Now we read the newspaper or listen to the radio to gather newsworthy facts. Many of us have applied these fact-gathering habits to our Bible reading as well, digging out facts about God and storing them for later use.

While learning information about God is important, we need more than this to form an interior, life-transforming relationship with God. What we need is reflection and interaction with God. Scripture meditation provides the opportunity to do this and ignites within us a powerful desire to respond to God as well as a desire for God.

And so Bible study is very different from Bible meditation. When we study, we dissect the text; when we meditate, we savor the text and enter into it. When we study, we ask questions about the text; when we meditate, we let the text ask questions of us. When we study, we read and compare facts and new ways of applying facts; when we meditate, we read to let God speak to us in light of the facts already absorbed.

In *Shaped by the Word,* Dr. Robert Mulholland of Asbury Seminary contrasts informational reading of Scripture with formational reading. His explanation of informational reading describes the way modern Christians often study the Bible. His explanation of formational reading describes the different approach needed for meditation.[1]

Informational Reading	Formational Reading
covering as much material as you can in a timely manner (getting to the end of the Bible chapter or book)	keeping a "holding pattern" over words or phrases that speak to you; your goal is not to finish a section, but to meet God
reading in a linear fashion, "moving quickly over the *surface of text*"	reading for depth, "open to multiple layers of meaning" and deeper dimensions
hoping to grasp the text and master it	allowing the text to master you
controlling the text and looking for what fits our systems of thought	hoping to be shaped by the text, we "stand before the text and await its address"
approaching words objectively and analytically	approaching words in a humble, detached, receptive way
hoping to find solutions to problems	maintaining openness to mystery and to whatever God may say

The informational approach puts the reader in charge, while the formational approach lets the Holy Spirit take charge. The informational approach often has the feel of conquering, while the formation-al approach is about resting in the text.

This phenomenon of resting in the text explains why teachers often get more out of the lesson than students—because they tend to *dwell* in the passage. While writing a Bible study session, I'd often find it living in me. During lunch break, I'd get more ideas about what God was saying in it to me. As I ran errands, it would come back to me and link up with other truths. At church the truth of it would stand out in the actions of a dear saint who otherwise considered himself a spiritu-al nobody. The truth of the passage would follow me everywhere because I'd sat in it and wrestled with it.

Meditation, then, builds the skill of hearing God at the heart and soul level. We learn to ask ourselves, *How do I respond deep within to this text? Why do I have these thoughts?* We ask these questions, believing that God is quite current in our lives and speaks to our broken places—some of which we are aware of and others we are not. Meditation challenges us to let an infinite, all-powerful God tiptoe into the messy realities of our lives and offer words of wisdom, comfort, and confrontation.

THE ROLE OF THE HOLY SPIRIT

Perhaps the idea of letting God speak directly to you—even through Scripture—seems beyond your understanding or even rather hocus-pocus. Yet all spiritual disciplines, including meditation, will be beyond your understanding because they are not *your* work alone. They are a result of the Holy Spirit at work in you as you connect with God.

In Scripture meditation the Holy Spirit has several roles, one of which is *author of Scripture:* "For prophecy never had its origin in the will of man, but men spoke from God as they were carried along by the Holy Spirit" (2 Peter 1:21). This is commonly referred to as the "inspiration" of the Scripture by the Holy Spirit.

Mulholland points out that inspiration is a two-fold process: God inspired the writing of the Scripture and also inspires our reading of the Scripture. So the Holy Spirit also has the role of *guide to truth,* as borne out by John 16:13: "But when he, the Spirit of truth, comes, he will guide you into all truth. He will not speak on his own; he will speak only what he hears, and he will tell you what is yet to come." Because Scripture is God-breathed, it is alive as we read it, thus having a "living and active" power; "sharper than any double-edged sword, it penetrates even to dividing soul and spirit, joints and marrow; it judges the thoughts and attitudes of the heart" (Hebrews 4:12).

The upshot of the Spirit's role is that when we meditate on Scripture, we can expect "a genuine encounter with God" because the Holy Spirit living in us connects with the Holy Spirit in the Scripture.[2] That wise old evangelical A. W. Tozer put it this way in *The Pursuit of God:* "[The Bible] is not only a book which was once spoken, but a book which is *now speaking.* . . . If you would follow on to know the Lord, come at once to the open Bible expecting it to speak to you."[3]

Because of this connection, it is wise to begin times of Scripture meditation with a prayer that God will enlighten us through the Spirit and reveal the Word *to us.* I forget this so easily that I often read a helpful reminder by Dietrich Bonhoeffer before meditating:

> In our meditation we ponder the chosen text on the strength of the promise that it has something utterly personal to say to us today and for our Christian life, that it is not only God's Word for the Church, but also God's Word for us individually. We expose ourselves to the specific word until it addresses us personally. And when we do this, we are doing no more than the simplest, untutored Christian does every day; we read God's Word as God's Word for us.[4]

The apostle Paul tells us that when we encounter the living Word of God, four things happen:

Teaching—letting the good news of Jesus Christ intrude in our life and radically change us

Reproof—letting God shine a light to discern our thoughts and intentions and reveal our places of brokenness

Correction—straightening out everything inconsistent in us with the full nature of God's joyous, loving being

Training—educating, nurturing, and growing us up into mature persons whose every action is a work of service to someone else[5]

When we add meditation to our habit of Bible study, we allow time for teaching, reproof, correction, and training to occur.

SURRENDERING TO THE TEXT

It seems to confuse people that meditation is not a matter of thinking hard about a text. It's about letting go and opening oneself to the text. Mulholland explains,

We have a deeply ingrained way of reading in which we are the masters of the material we read. We come to a text with our own agenda firmly in place, perhaps not always consciously but usually subconsciously. If what we start to read does not quickly begin to adapt itself to our agenda [solving problems, answering questions], we usually lay it aside and look for something that does. When what we are reading does adapt itself to our agenda, we analyze, critique, dissect, reorganize, synthesize, and digest the material. Thus our general mode of reading is to perceive the text as an object "out there" over which we have control.

*We control our approach to the text; we control our interaction with
the text; we control the impact of the text upon our lives.*[6]

An informational approach to reading Proverbs would be to look for
wise instruction about a certain topic, such as money or friendship. This
is a helpful, valid method of Bible study. But a formational approach
would be to read a small portion at a time, opening your mind and heart
to whatever God may say to you today. Both approaches are needed.

Self-surrender is central in our life with God, and meditating on
Scripture teaches us surrender. We may have studied the text before,
but when we let go of our agenda for the text and of preconceived ideas
about what the text might mean to us today, we truly open ourselves to
what God wants us to know and to feel convicted about.

In fact it can be difficult to meditate on a passage we know very
well. In college I heard an excellent sermon on Philippians 4:4-8. For
thirty years I have remembered and been enriched by the four-point
outline I heard that day. But I found it difficult to meditate on that passage. There was no room to let God speak to me today because I
already knew what God had said to me yesterday. But with every passage, I need to allow God to speak to me based on where I am today. If
you are open to God, God may surprise you and speak to you about a
problem you thought was solved, a relationship you thought had healed,
or a conclusion you've already made. Even if you were right about the
problem, relationship, or conclusion, you may, through meditation (or
afterward), see the heart of the other party and experience a mercy you
didn't have before.

In meditation we often have our false self stripped away and our
true self revealed—that we care a great deal about what other people
think of us or that our possessions mean more to us than we thought.
Under normal circumstances this would be painful and embarrassing,

but in meditation we have yielded ourselves to the hands of the Potter, who is safe and will do the molding without breaking us. We get a sense of God having seen through us, having loved us deeply, and having called us to something better. We taste and see that God is good. Our character changes because we have a new vision of God and of how God calls us to participate in a kingdom of goodness and obedience.

MEDITATION IS NOT APPLICATION

To meditate on a passage is not to ask oneself, *How does this apply to me?* Application is the common-sense reflection, *Where in my work, family life, finances, health, or relationship with God do I need the principles of this passage?* This is an excellent question to ask and it takes prayer and thought to figure out possible answers. That's why it helps to discuss application in a class.

Meditation, however, is different. You stop thinking so hard and wait for God to speak. The closest you come to application might be asking, *How does this passage intersect with my life?* But you're asking God, not yourself. The kind of question to ask in meditation is, *What does the idea that stands out to me in this passage have to do with a certain person or circumstance?* If nothing else, ask God, *What do I need to know today about my life with you?* Immediate answers probably will not come, but questions will open you up to an ongoing conversation with God all day, knowing that the answers may come even out of the lips of children and infants (see Psalm 8:2).

The difference is that application is analysis, that helpful left-brain activity where you connect the dots between the principle of the passage and, for instance, how you behave behind the wheel of your car. But meditation is right-brained and intuitive. You let go and listen. You hear what you need to know either during the quiet of meditation or later. On the other hand, just because meditation is more intuitive, you will not be overwhelmed with nonstop flashes of insight. Meditation is a skill that left-brained people benefit from as they learn to let go of all the voices in their mind that analyze situations and tell them what to do.

The effect of meditation is different too. Instead of forcing yourself to change your behavior, you let the Spirit invite you to imitate that rich, broad character of God. An analogy from my college days might help illustrate this concept. The Christian college I graduated from had an early, strict curfew. Even though the curfew details and reasons were explained fully to me, I responded with much eye rolling and eventually was restricted to my room for one weekend for violating the curfew. I continued to whine about the curfew until I had an unusual conversation with the dorm mother. In a typical late-teen crisis over a boyfriend, I knocked on her door and she invited me in. We sat in her living room and I spilled a few details. We sat in the quiet for a few minutes. Then she looked at me with great love and intensity and began talking about how she had struggled in my situation. She told me a story from her teens of an incident she regretted (so innocent that I almost burst out laughing). But I could see the purity of heart in her face and posture, and it called forth the same in me. After that I never broke curfew or even thought about it. I even stopped griping about it.

My visit with the dorm mother affected me the way meditation does. Before, I'd been given rules and handy suggestions. I was told to cooperate. I didn't. But after being listened to and loved by a woman who read the unstated struggle in my mind and challenged me by the goodness of her life, I no longer had to work so hard to be obedient. I *wanted* to do the good and right thing. In meditation God sits with us in the quiet and speaks to us personally. Because the encounter is so relational, we are never the same.

Here's an example of how the processes and outcomes of application and meditation differ. Recently, I came to Hosea 2 in my walk through the Prophets. Those seeking to apply the passage would notice that Gomer (and metaphorically, the nation of Israel) had many things in life that made her forget God: lovers, food, water, wool, linen, oil, drink (see verse 5). Then they might quiz themselves about what their idols are. They'd probably come up with the usual suspects: possessions, career, appearance, health-consciousness, leisure, even family members. They might close by making promises to God about those issues.

But because I also meditated, I set aside those ideas for a while and tried to stay completely open to the text. I sat quietly and waited. The words *wilderness* and *parched* stood out to me (see Hosea 2:3). I reread the passage, noting those words, and could see that Gomer was lost and desolate. I sat in the place of Gomer, and to my surprise I felt her fears. Within a few seconds I also felt my own fears about an upcoming speaking trip abroad. It held such possibilities for travel glitches, personality clashes, and feelings of inadequacy. I hadn't realized I was so unnerved. Because I wanted to avoid living Gomer's wandering and parched life, I responded by praying about staying nourished and nurtured by God while I was away. I asked God what that would look like. Several helpful ideas came to me that I'd never considered before: I packed copies of my favorite classic works of Madame Guyon and Brother Lawrence; I took flavored decaf coffee, which so often accompanies my hanging-out-with-God moments at home; instead of thinking I was too well traveled to need the herbal remedy for jet-lag that was recommended, I ordered it. I sat a while longer, verbalizing my trust in God, and a favorite scriptural image came to me: I could sit beside those still waters, even in that distant country (see Psalm 23:2).

How Bible Study
Enhances Meditation

To meditate is not to forgo or degrade Bible study. In fact, study prepares us to meditate on a passage, acting as step 1 to meditation, which is step 2. Studying the historical, linguistic, and cultural facts behind a passage as well as the context provides clues to what was intended by the writer of the text. Within that accurate textual rendering, we can meditate with more discernment. Then we're more likely to comprehend what God is saying to us at this moment of life. Here are some examples of how study helps.

Historical Information

Knowing who King Uzziah was helps us understand the dramatic episode of Isaiah 6, where Isaiah saw the Lord on the throne, with a train so huge it filled the temple. When the six-winged seraphs (these are fun to picture!) sang, "Holy, holy, holy is the LORD Almighty; the whole earth is full of his glory," the temple shook violently and smoke filled the room (verse 3). (Once, when I pictured this, I remembered a Christian concert where a machine filled the huge arena with smoke.) In the height of this drama, Isaiah saw (or had an intuition) of his own sinfulness: "'Woe to me!' I cried. 'I am ruined! For I am a man of unclean lips, and I live among a people of unclean lips, and my eyes have seen the King, the LORD Almighty'" (verse 5). This in turn changed his life and launched him into his prophetic career.

Knowing about King Uzziah deepens our understanding during meditation because Uzziah was one of the best kings Judah ever had. When Uzziah died, Isaiah's easy life was over. Now Judah needed a strong prophet, and Isaiah needed to step up to the plate. This shows us the ways of God. God rarely calls us out of the blue one day with a vision. More likely we view tragedies and miracles around us and, while seeking God, God makes it clear what we're to do in response. The day I meditated on this passage, I asked God, "What tragedies and miracles are occurring around me? How are you calling me to respond?"

CONTEXT

Parallel passages and related passages enlighten us with details about persons or situations, especially their past. In Matthew 20:20-28, James and John and "Mama Thunder" (my nickname for their mother) came to Jesus, asking that the two men sit on the right and left of Jesus when he came into his kingdom. Jesus asked them two questions: "What is it you want?" and "Can you drink the cup I am going to drink?" They told him what they wanted and then answered the second question: "We can."

Watching their boldness takes on a dramatic cast when you know the timing of the discussion and what became of these folks. This discussion occurred not long before Jesus' death. The disciples were on their way to Jerusalem, where Jesus' enemies were planning to kill him. Because the showdown was imminent, these three may have thought this was their last chance to approach Jesus. Their requests created a rousing discussion among the disciples, and Jesus responded by teaching that his disciples would humble themselves, not exalt themselves.

The near future of James and John is key. Not long after this, in the garden of Gethsemane, Jesus kept these two brothers and Peter near him while he prayed. While this might have been for comfort (which they didn't provide because they fell asleep), Jesus also probably did this because even in their drowsiness they needed to hear him pray about "the cup" he was going to drink. Within hours they refused the cup of suffering by deserting him and hiding. All of their boasting would shortly come back to haunt them.

Once when I was meditating on this passage, I became very upset by the two questions Jesus asked. In response to "What is it you want?" I knew I wanted to let a few people know how mistaken they were about something good my husband (their pastor) had done. I would soon be in a place where I could easily correct their misconception. My husband didn't want me to do this, but I wanted to fix things. I'd been trying to wrangle from God a divine go-ahead to do so.

Then I meditated on the second question about drinking the cup Jesus drank. From the context of Scripture, I knew that cup was the cup of suffering. I didn't like being asked to suffer! Finally, I became upset because I saw myself being as pushy as Mama Thunder had been. I did not want to be like her, but I was. I got curious about her future, wondering if she had been present at the crucifixion. If so, she would have witnessed the horror of it and known this foreshadowed horror for her sons (James, a martyr's death; John, a persecuted and exiled life). I thought, *If she drank that cup of suffering (watching the crucifixion), I would drink my cup of being silent instead of defending my husband.* Rising from my place of meditation, I searched further in the Bible to find Mama Thunder standing there with Mary by the cross (see Matthew 27:56). I decided to stand alongside her too and drink my cup. I would let my reputation suffer without anyone knowing the good my husband had done.

Read this passage about power, position, and respectability for yourself (see Matthew 20:20-28, below). Don't rush or glide through it in sleep mode. Pay attention to these real people. Then shut your eyes and imagine James, John, and Mama Thunder talking to Jesus. Let Jesus ask you the two questions (in nonitalic type). Sit quietly and ask God, "Is there anything I need to know today?" If you get involved and don't finish reading this chapter, that's okay. Finish it later.

Then the mother of Zebedee's sons came to Jesus with her sons and, kneeling down, asked a favor of him.

"What is it you want?" *he asked.*

She said, "Grant that one of these two sons of mine may sit at your right and the other at your left in your kingdom."

"You don't know what you are asking," Jesus said to them. "Can you drink the cup I am going to drink?"

"We can," they answered.

Jesus said to them, "You will indeed drink from my cup, but to sit at my right or left is not for me to grant. These places belong to those for whom they have been prepared by my Father."

When the ten heard about this, they were indignant with the two brothers. Jesus called them together and said, "You know that the rulers of the Gentiles lord it over them, and their high officials exercise authority over them. Not so with you. Instead, whoever wants to become great among you must be your servant, and whoever wants to be first must be your slave—just as the Son of Man did not come to be served, but to serve, and to give his life as a ransom for many." (Emphasis added.)

CULTURAL INFORMATION

To meditate on Mark 1:40-45, you may need to know something about leprosy. In biblical times, leprosy included several skin ailments, many of which were contagious and incurable. Some resulted in paralysis and gangrene. Old Testament law did not allow lepers to participate in social and religious activities, and those who touched lepers were considered "unclean" (see Leviticus 13–14). Jews saw leprosy as a sign of God's curse and some threw rocks at lepers to keep them away.

But Jesus was not as careful as doctors, dentists, and nurses are today, who protect themselves by wearing gloves and masks. Mark wrote, "Filled with compassion, Jesus reached out his hand and touched the man" (verse 41). Jesus seemed to know the need people had for human touch because in many of his healings he touched them. He wanted to heal not just the body but the entire soul. Understandably, the leper had been reticent: "*If you are willing,* you can make me clean." Jesus answered with the compassionate touch and the words "I am willing" (verses 40-41, emphasis added). So often was Jesus "filled with compassion," you have to wonder if he wasn't in tears at times as he healed.

Put yourself in Jesus' place as he touched this man. He would have felt the boils and lesions. What feelings would this evoke in you? What feelings do you imagine Jesus' touch evoked in this leprous man? Remember that people who are not often touched have what is called "skin hunger." They are starved for touch.

Read the passage now and reflect on these details, as well as what Jesus had to give up after healing the man.

> *A man with leprosy came to him and begged him on his knees, "If you are willing, you can make me clean."*
>
> *Filled with compassion, Jesus reached out his hand and touched the man. "I am willing," he said. "Be clean!" Immediately the leprosy left him and he was cured.*
>
> *Jesus sent him away at once with a strong warning: "See that you don't tell this to anyone. But go, show yourself to the priest and offer the sacrifices that Moses commanded for your cleansing, as a testimony to them." Instead he went out and began to talk freely, spreading the news. As a result, Jesus could no longer enter a town openly but stayed outside in lonely places. Yet the people still came to him from everywhere.*

Ponder how Jesus behaved in this passage. (You don't have to close your eyes and so on.) What does it make you want to say back to God?

SETTING

First, read this passage:

> *If you have any encouragement from being united with Christ, if any comfort from his love, if any fellowship with the Spirit, if any tenderness and compassion, then make my joy complete by being like-minded, having the same love, being one in spirit and purpose. Do nothing out of selfish ambition or vain conceit, but in humility consider others better than yourselves. Each of you should look not only to your own interests, but also to the interests of others. . . .*
>
> *Do everything without complaining or arguing, so that you may become blameless and pure, children of God without fault in a crooked and depraved generation, in which you shine like stars in the universe as you hold out the word of life—in order that I may boast on the day of Christ that I did not run or labor for nothing.*
> *(Philippians 2:1-4,14-16)*

Now consider where the first readers of this passage lived: Philippi. Philippi was a Roman colony and the leading city of the district of Macedonia. Named for Philip of Macedon (master of Greece and father of Alexander the Great), Philippi focused on trade and getting ahead. Paul's words about humility and unity must have been radical!

Now picture the listeners. If they were still meeting where Paul and Silas first taught them, they were outside the city gate by the river—beyond the watchful eyes of city officials. According to Acts 16:12-40, the Christians there included:

- *a prison jailer (middle-class civil servant) who, when he thought Paul had escaped, had almost killed himself, but Paul stopped him. He and his family were subsequently baptized*
- *a rich fabric merchandiser, Lydia, with whom Paul and Silas stayed*
- *a slave girl fortune-teller, who had been demon-possessed*

Visitors might have included

- *the slave girl's owners, who had had Paul and Silas arrested*
- *members of the crowd, who attacked Paul and Silas*
- *those who beat Paul and Silas*
- *town officials, who ordered them to be stripped and beaten and later found out they were Roman citizens and tried to appease them*

Which of these hearers would you have wanted to associate with? Which ones might have frightened you?

Read the passage again and put yourself in the place of the hearers. Who would have been most difficult for you to "consider better than yourself" The slave girl? Those who beat Paul and Silas? The town officials who ordered it done?

Then shut your eyes and ask God, "How are you asking me to change today?" Don't try to invent any insights. Just rest in God.

Questions and Activities for Individual Reflection or Group Discussion
1. What, if anything, was said in this chapter that has made you think?

2. When have you had an experience of being loved into obedience (similar to the dorm mom story)?

3. Imagine yourself sitting down to read a chapter of Scripture. If you were to approach the text thinking that the Holy Spirit not only inspired it many years ago but also inspires you as you read it now, how would that change your attitude in reading?

4. Go back to one of these passages and ponder one of them further:

>   Isaiah 6:1-8—Isaiah seeing the Lord on the throne
>   Matthew 20:20-28—Mama Thunder, James, and John seeking
>   position
>   Mark 1:40-45—Jesus healing the man with leprosy
>   Philippians 2:1-4,14-16—exploring humility with high and low society

Group leader instructions for question 4: As a group, figure out which of the four passages most of you did not already meditate on individually. Use that passage and then, as a group, quiet yourselves and shut your eyes. Have a group member read the passage aloud and wait in silence. The leader should ask members to open their eyes and take turns *briefly* answering this question: *What word or phrase or scene or moment emerges from the passage and stays with you?*

With eyes shut, reflect a while longer and consider if God is offering you an invitation in this passage to enlarge your understanding or to do something in the next few days. Ponder this question: *What do I need to know from this passage?*

After a while, group members open their eyes and those who wish can *briefly* offer their answer to the second question.

Close in prayer, asking God to help the group members interact with God personally as they learn to meditate.

Chapter Four

INVITING GOD TO
SPEAK TO YOU

PRACTICAL GUIDELINES FOR MEDITATION

When a man in his eighties who I knew had a long and rich history with God participated in one of my meditation workshops, I wondered what else he might possibly need to hear from God. The passage for the session was 1 Kings 19, when Elijah wants to die and then goes on his long journey only to hear God's gentle whisper outside a cave.

After the session this very Christlike man stopped me and told me he'd heard God tell him to come out of that cave and stand in the presence of the Lord; his age was keeping him in the cave. Furthermore he, like Elijah, had a successor to anoint and he needed to actively pour himself into that person.

As we invite God to speak to us as we meditate on Scripture, sometimes we have a revolutionary and poignant encounter like this man did. Other times we simply pay attention and stay alert for what God says through the Word and how that impacts our life today. In either case, *openness* and *practice* are essential to hearing from God.

Helpful Hints

Perhaps as you've attempted to meditate, you've found it's easier to become absorbed in the meditation experience at certain times and you've wondered why. Here are some basic hints that those experienced in meditation have found to be helpful. (Further guidelines for group meditation are found in appendix A.)

Find a Good Location and Body Position

Choose a place that is quiet, restful, and comfortable. Use the same place every day, if possible. Many people recommend a special place where you do nothing but solitary disciplines such as prayer and meditation. That isn't possible for everyone, so find out what works for you and do it. Disconnect the telephone if necessary.

Position your body so you won't be distracted or uncomfortable. Those practiced in meditation advise sitting in a straight-back chair, placing feet flat on the floor and hands on the knees or gently clasped. Crossing arms or legs necessitates uncrossing or causes limbs to fall asleep, which can be distracting.

On the other hand, people meditate in many positions: sitting on the floor against a wall so that the head is supported and legs lie resting in front; lying on the floor on their back or on their face; sitting in a chair with legs propped up in a chair facing them. The point is to find a position in which you can get settled, and stay there.

Pause and Breathe

We spend all day responding to stimuli—answering the telephone, following schedules, evaluating what needs to be done next. When it's quiet, these activities become "traffic" in our heads that keeps us from focusing on God. To interrupt this traffic, we can focus on being present in the moment by breathing in and out deeply, even in an exaggerated way. After meditating for years, I thought I didn't need to do this anymore. But I still do.

Relax

After taking several slow, deep breaths, relax body parts one by one: bend the neck, let the arms go limp, relax the legs and ankles. Loosen each part from the inside out. No matter how practiced you are, this is important. As you let go of tension, you prepare yourself to let go of your control over the text and what you think God might say to you. Relaxed stillness is an outward rehearsal of inward surrender.

Turn Over Distracting Thoughts to God

Surrender the numerous thoughts that distract you. The following exercise from Richard Foster's *Celebration of Discipline* has helped many people surrender interrupting thoughts to God.

> Begin by placing your palms down as a symbolic indication of your desire to turn over any concerns you may have to God. Inwardly you may pray, "Lord, I give to you my anger toward John. I release my fear of my dentist appointment this morning. I surrender my anxiety over not having enough money to pay the bills this month. I release my frustration over trying to find a baby-sitter for tonight."
> Whatever it is that weighs on your mind or is a concern to you, just say, "palms down." Release it. After several moments of surrender, turn your palms up as a symbol of your desire to receive from God. Perhaps you will pray silently: "Lord, I would like to receive your

*divine love for John, your peace about the dentist appointment, your
patience, your joy."*[1]

ASK FOR GUIDANCE FROM THE HOLY SPIRIT

Begin with a prayer inviting the Holy Spirit to reveal God's Word
to you. Then quiet your thoughts and focus on the passage.

But don't be too concerned about technique. Concentrate rather
on how reading the Bible is like reading a letter from a loved one. So
after we read, we "linger over words, savor them and allow them to soak
into the very center of our being," as Dietrich Bonhoeffer said.[2]

THE IMPORTANCE OF RESPONDING

Beware of thinking of meditation as a nice little experience in
which God wows you. God's goal in our interaction with Scripture is
not that we'll feel tingly now and then. God is aiming for the transformation of our souls, for us to become the kind of persons our
mother and our spouse and our coworkers have prayed we would
please become! So view meditation as part of your ongoing interactive
dialogue with God. Don't walk away from meditation without
responding to God.

Typically, this response is prayer. Eighteenth-century reformer
William Law counseled, "When in reading Scripture you meet with a
passage that seems to give your heart a new motion toward God, turn
it into the form of a petition, and give it a place in your prayers."[3] That
petition may be to pray, "O God, I see what you're saying to me. What
is it you want me to do in response?" Or that prayer may simply express
thankfulness that God's "desire is to give Himself to the soul that really

loves Him and to that soul which earnestly seeks Him," according to Madame Jeanne Guyon.[4]

You may find yourself responding by celebrating. You can sing or do a little dance or play an instrument. Or you may be confused enough to ask God, "What is the invitation in this passage? What does this tell me about you? What are you really getting at?" In some cases you may respond by lying on the floor and weeping.

A common prayerlike response is to pull out paper and scribble your thoughts. In this sort of journaling, you address God directly, responding to what God has said to you. Journaling can be especially helpful when your thoughts are jumbled and you need clarity to pray. Choosing words clarifies our thoughts and helps us realize we've stretched a point or eluded a confrontation.

If journaling intimidates you, call it scribbling. Just jot down what's going through your head and what you'd like to say to God if you were to pray. Or simply write your prayer and address God directly. Remember that the secret of authentic journaling is to write with the supposition that no one else will ever see it. Then you are more likely to let the Holy Spirit reveal your real self to you. (And you're free to tear it up when you're done.) This authenticity shows in David's "journaling" of Psalm 59. He wrote out the feelings and need for trust "when Saul had sent men to watch David's house in order to kill him" (in introduction to Psalm). The result was a grisly psalm that brought David to a place of obedience and nonretaliation against Saul.

Some people shy away from journaling because they see it as a taskmaster—an obligation to fulfill every day. This is not true. You can journal as needed. Journaling, like all spiritual disciplines, follows the principle Christ applied to the discipline of Sabbath keeping: people weren't created for their journals; journaling was created for people (from Mark 2:27). So when you feel the urge to confess, to grieve, to rejoice, to surrender, act on it. Pouring out this response before God on paper helps you find your center in God.

WHAT YOU CAN EXPECT TO HEAR

Times of meditation will turn out to be quite practical. As you meditate on Scripture, the Holy Spirit will bring up names, faces, and situations over which the truth of this Scripture needs to come to bear. Expect to change your ideas about relationships and decisions.

You will probably sense something different from the same passage each time you meditate on it. That's because each day you experience different insights about God, different feelings, and different puzzlements about life. Last week you would never have noticed the phrase that shimmers for you today, because today your circumstances are different.

Another reason we hear differently than last week or last month is that we hear God in themes. If you took a class or had a conversation or read a book that challenged you, don't be surprised if in meditation you "hear" a message related to that theme. Ask yourself how it amplifies or perhaps contradicts what you've already been hearing. Such pondering helps us connect the dots between ideas and expands our thinking.

Other times what comes to us in meditation comes "out of the blue." Many of our thoughts are hidden to us, but meditation reveals them. Dallas Willard wrote, "We usually know very little about the things that move in our soul, the deepest level of our life, or what is driving it. Our 'within' is astonishingly complex and subtle."[5] Meditation speaks to those hidden thoughts and brings them forward. This is why it's wise to continually pray, "Search me, O God, and know my heart; test me and know my anxious thoughts. See if there is any offensive way in me, and lead me in the way everlasting" (Psalm 139:23-24).

During a workshop on meditation, an attractive, late-fortyish woman named Kathy had an unexpected insight after we meditated on the parable of the lost sheep. In it the word *rejoice* had stood out to her. She'd also pictured neighbors coming to a party and realized that the party was a wedding—not hers, but her sister's. "My sister and I are both single," she told the group, "so I was jealous. How had my sister ended up with the man of her dreams, but I didn't? In this passage, God was telling me to rejoice anyway. So I prayed and God said to me, 'Kathy, I have the finest things saved for you too. Don't fear that you'll never meet the man of your dreams. I'll take care of you. Give up this fear.'"

Kathy said that prior to this she hadn't realized how much this fear had ruled her. As she further meditated on what had come to her in the passage, she dealt with this core fear she'd been burying.

God often speaks through Scripture this way. We hesitate to believe it, however, for fear of misinterpreting the text. That fear comes from hearing people force a point-by-point allegory on a passage. Often this is done to try to divine what action they are to do next. We balk at this because it's like using Scripture as a Ouija board, hoping for a spontaneous secret message from God. This is as silly as opening the Bible, shutting your eyes, and landing a finger on the name of the person you're supposedly to marry.

Instead, in meditation we perceive the personality of Jesus or other redeemed ones and consider what God is calling us to *be.* The issues we discern in meditation are about what sort of heart we are to have, based on what we see in the heart of God or Jesus. Only after we've cultivated that heart of Christ will it be clear to us what we are to *do* next.

Meditation makes life an adventure because our interactive life with God grows. Each day presents new possibilities for the divine drama of what God will say to us and lead us to do. If we don't respond well, God shows us how to respond better and invites us to be alert for "take two."

Questions and Activities for Individual Reflection or Group Discussion

1.   What, if anything, was said in this chapter that has made you think?

2.   Which of the guidelines do you think will be most helpful to you?

> *Location and body position*
> *Pause and breathe*
> *Relax*
> *Turn over distracting thoughts to God*
> *Ask for guidance from the Holy Spirit*

3.   How do we miss out if we don't respond to God in some way—asking God questions, giving thanks, pondering our next step, celebrating, weeping?

4.   Try the following *guided meditation* on Mark 5:25-34. (A guided meditation is one in which a leader guides you through a passage of Scripture, adding details that help you meditate but pausing to let you picture the events or words of the passage for yourself.) You'll be your own leader, which means you'll silently read the leader's directions and do as instructed. Read the reader's part aloud and keep reading and following the leader's instructions and the instructions in brackets.

Group leader instructions for question 4: Even if group members did the guided meditation on their own, try it as a group. You'll need one group member to be the *reader* and another to be the *leader*. The reader reads the Scripture and the leader reads the instructions and follows the directions regarding what to say aloud (in quotation marks). Both follow the instructions in brackets.

Leader: "The reader will read parts of Mark 5:25-34 and pause. Then I will ask you questions and pause for you to reflect. I invite you to shut your eyes and enjoy being discipled by Jesus." [Pause] "Be still and know that God is God." [Pause and then pray] "Oh God, send the Holy Spirit to us through the Word. Reveal your Word to us. Lord Jesus, bless the hearing of the words of this passage."

Reader: "And a woman was there who had been subject to bleeding for twelve years. She had suffered a great deal under the care of many doctors and had spent all she had, yet instead of getting better she grew worse."

Leader: "Put yourself in the place of this woman. How do you view yourself? Because you are unclean, no one has hugged you or touched you for years." [Pause for at least one full minute, if not more.] "How do you feel about doctors?"

Reader: "When she heard about Jesus, she came up behind him in the crowd and touched his cloak, because she thought, 'If I just touch his clothes, I will be healed.'"

Leader: "Where are you getting the nerve to even touch this rabbi's clothes?"

Reader: "Immediately her bleeding stopped and she felt in her body that she was freed from her suffering."

Leader: "How does it feel in your body to have your illness gone in a flash?" [Pause] "How does your face feel now?"

Reader: "At once Jesus realized that power had gone out from him. He turned around in the crowd and asked, 'Who touched my clothes?' 'You see the people crowding against you,' his disciples answered, 'and yet you can ask, "Who touched me?"' But Jesus kept looking around to see who had done it."

Leader: "When you heard the words, 'Who touched me?' what went through your mind?" [Pause] "As Jesus looks through the crowd, do you want him to find you? Are you afraid or do you want him to find you?"

Reader: "Then the woman, knowing what had happened to her, came and fell at his feet and, trembling with fear, told him the whole truth. He said to her, 'Daughter, your faith has healed you. Go in peace and be freed from your suffering.'"

Leader: "How does it feel to have the courage to tell the 'whole truth' about your gynecological disorder in a group of Palestinian men?" [Pause] "How does it feel to have Jesus—a rabbi who is not supposed to talk to women in public—call you by that endearing term *Daughter*?" [Pause] "I invite you to respond to God: What is God calling you to be? You may want to sit with your eyes closed or write for a while. Ask yourself, 'What is God saying to me? What do I want to say to God?'" [Pause for at least five minutes, longer if your group is experienced at meditation.] "Form a short three- or four-word prayer response to God, perhaps, 'Thank you for . . .' or, 'Show me how . . .'" [Pause and then pray] "Thank you, O God, that you come to us and speak to us."

Chapter Five

HEARING GOD WELL IN MEDITATION

OVERCOMING OBSTACLES TO HEARING GOD'S VOICE

When we try to meditate, the major difficulty seems to be quieting our-selves. Normally, we are plugged into headphones, tuned into the radio, transfixed with a book, or mesmerized by a TV show. Not so with med-itation. It thrives on silence, and that takes some adjustment.

Being creatures of such a culture, we usually find one of two things happening to us when we sit quietly. One is that we fall asleep. If this happens to you, God bless you in that time of rest. You must have need-ed it. Hurried, stressed-out folks do need sleep. The other common thing that happens is that our minds race, making lists of things we have to do and people we have to contact. If that happens to you, consider keeping a pen and paper nearby and jot down "to do" items that dis-tract you—errands to run, people to call. As you list each one, con-sciously release it to God.

Perhaps the silence makes you uncomfortable. But hearing God in

Scripture requires that we welcome silence, understanding it's a time of great fertility and growth, not of emptiness. Madeleine L'Engle compares meditation to planting onion bulbs in the ground: "They go down into the ground into silence, and they stay there in the silence and in the dark. And then these little green shoots come up. I think it is the same way with us spiritually, putting things down in the dark and letting them grow."[1]

Silence also cultivates vulnerability toward God, because silence is an outward form of inward surrender. Being able to quiet oneself is the secret to hearing God well in meditation. Dallas Willard puts it this way: "Nine-tenths of meditation is ignoring things, letting stuff go. It's the art of purposefully allowing stuff to drop off."[2]

Learning to quiet ourselves not only helps us meditate but also enhances our spiritual life. How? So much of transformation is about relinquishing to God things we cannot control. As we learn inner quiet, we're free to focus on the persons or things in front of us instead of hurrying and being distracted by urgent tasks. We're better in relationships because we care deeply about the people standing in front of us and listen intently to them instead of worrying about saying the right thing or winning someone to our side. In silence we learn to set our minds and hearts on God, to become fully preoccupied with God.

Staying Focused on God

Distractions usually come from feeling we have to finish our meditation so we can move on. In our hurry we gloss over words of Scripture, not reading them as if every word is God-breathed for our benefit. When this happens, consider if one of the following needs to be addressed.

PRAY ABOUT ISSUES THAT DISTRACT YOUR THOUGHTS

Don't scold yourself when your mind wanders, but gently include your distracting thoughts in your prayer.

> *Our thoughts are likely to wander and go their own way toward*
> *other persons or to some events in our life. Much as this may distress*
> *and shame us again and again, we must not lose heart and become*
> *anxious, or even conclude that meditation is really not something for*
> *us. When this happens it is often a help not to snatch back our*
> *thoughts convulsively, but quite calmly to incorporate into our prayer*
> *the people and events to which our thoughts keep straying and thus in*
> *all patience return to the starting point of the meditation.*[3]

If certain thoughts are particularly disruptive, journal about them to examine what's behind them and get them out of your system. Write honestly: Here's what I'm afraid of today. Here's what I feel incapable of tackling today. Here's an upcoming event that I would rather skip, and here's why. The psalmist did this: "Every morning you'll hear me at it again. Every morning I lay out the pieces of my life on your altar and watch for fire to descend" (Psalm 5:3, MSG).

CHOOSE A BETTER TIME OF DAY

The authors of *Prayer and Temperament* wrote, "Choose the time of the day when we are most alert, least distracted, least tired, most well-rested, and without outside pressure."[4] Most people recommend you do this first thing when you arise. While this is optimal, it doesn't work for many people, and forcing ourselves to do it makes it less likely to work.

If you're not a morning person and it doesn't work for you, choose another time when you are relaxed and clearheaded. When I first began meditating, I chose the time just after lunch. I'd already broken my work routine and I felt relaxed.

Choose the Scripture Text Purposefully

The process of hunting to discover the text for the day is distracting, so have a plan to follow. You may use a recommended list (such as a lectionary, which contains the Scripture texts used each week in church services of certain denominations around the world) or stay with a theme (such as Jesus' healings) or simply work through a book of the Bible. Ten verses or fewer a day is sufficient. Your goal is not to get through the book but to interact with God. Bonhoeffer prescribed that "in our personal meditation we confine ourselves to a brief selected text, which possibly may not be changed for a whole week."[5]

However, be open to shifting your plans now and then. For two years I worked through Old Testament Prophets with great joy. But the summer my mother died, I switched to meditating through the gospel of Mark. I needed familiar passages that kept me close to Jesus. Later I went back to the Prophets. If you've just read or heard riveting teaching about a passage, you may wish to switch to it for a while. That happened to me recently with Song of Songs and later with Psalm 119. I spent a few weeks in each and then went back to my plan.

Consider the centrality of the Gospels. Francis de Sales, Bishop of Geneva in the early seventeenth century and author of *Introduction to the Devout Life,* was well practiced in meditation and advised, "I especially counsel you to practice mental prayer, the prayer of the heart, and particularly that which centers on the life and passion of our Lord. By often turning your eyes on him in meditation, your whole soul will be filled with him. You will learn his ways and form your actions after the pattern of his."[6] Meditating on Gospel passages helps you get to know the character and personality of Jesus. Then you're more likely to know what Jesus would say or do in any given situation in your life.

In the beginning especially, it's wise to choose texts that answer the conscious needs of your soul, especially your places of brokenness. For example, those sensing they don't truly believe God loves them may want to meditate on passages that mention God delighting in us, such as:

> *"The LORD your God is with you, he is mighty to save. He will take*
> *great delight in you, he will quiet you with his love, he will rejoice*
> *over you with singing" (Zephaniah 3:17).*
> *"He brought me out into a spacious place; he rescued me because he*
> *delighted in me" (Psalm 18:19).*

You may wish to use a concordance or topical Bible to find pertinent passages. I found the previous references by looking for the word *delight* in such reference books. Then I studied the passages and began meditating on them.

If you have been a people pleaser for years—doing what others want you to do while giving little attention to God's call on your life— you might meditate on Matthew 10:26-31. In this passage the phrase "do not be afraid" occurs three times. Each occurrence deals with being afraid of what others think. Focus also on the second part of verse 28, in which Jesus spoke of being afraid of God. What does it mean to have a holy, healthy fear of God? Isn't it silly *not* to tremble before the creator of the universe? If we have such a healthy fear of God, how does that affect our thoughts about pleasing others? Won't others' opinions cease to matter as much when God becomes the object of our longing? How would it feel to have this holy, healthy fear of God?

Recognize the Voices on Your "Committee"

You will make great progress in hearing God in Scripture and all of life if you know and recognize the voices of the "committee" that lives in your head. An important part of our spiritual life is "letting go of all that resists" God,[7] and the committee members in your head are your worst interrupters. They often try to imitate God so that you think you're hearing God when you're really only hearing a broken part of your soul. Get to know each one and what each is crying out for. Here are some possibilities:

The looking-good kid—*This is the part of your unregenerated self that desperately wants to be loved and valued. He or she works hard to be admired out of fear of not being good enough. If you've been rejected before, this committee member makes sure it won't happen again. If you think you hear God saying, "Be perfect! Get it right! Don't make any mistakes—then I'll be proud of you!" this is not God, but your looking-good kid. It sabotages every Scripture passage, making it seem to be about being better and working harder.*

The kickback kid—*This part of you is afraid you'll be forgotten, so he or she entertains others in order to feel loved. He thinks of something fun you could do instead of meditate. She is usually afraid of success because that would mean buckling down and being responsible. The primary thought is, If I don't ever try, I won't ever fail.*

The rescuer—*This committee member is the broken part of you that also wants to be loved and valued, so he or she helps others so much that they have to love you. As a result, busyness is next to godliness. If you think you hear God saying in every passage, "Help people until it exhausts you. Make people happy," that is not God but your rescuer sabotaging your meditation.*

The attitude police—*This committee member wants everything done right! He or she evaluates, criticizes, and ruins your attempts to focus on God. The attitude police sabotages your meditation so that every passage is a correction of you or of someone else.*

The grouch—*This is the part of you that feels sorry for yourself and demands the attention of others. It infiltrates the Scripture to say, "You blew it again. Get with it! Nothing is ever going to work for you."*

Your committee may also include a proud and tyrannical parent, an overbearing boss, a clown, a daredevil, a promiscuous flirt, or a maverick intellectual. It's important to name your committee members before God so you can surrender these false or broken parts of yourself. They are the parts of your soul not yet transformed, which are deeply influenced by the enemy of your soul.

Fighting with committee members doesn't work. It works better to recognize them for who they are and gently escort them to the door of your heart. Also look for passages that speak to these broken parts of your soul. Let Scripture say to your looking-good kid: God sees your failures and delights in you anyway. To your kickback kid: God gives courage and confidence. To your rescuer: God shows up in every catastrophe. Sometimes God asks you to come along; other times, you stay behind. To your attitude police: God fixes the world. You pray and love. To the grouch: God loves you, no matter what. God never gives up on you.

The more skilled you become in quieting yourself, the easier meditation becomes. It takes discipline at first, but once you begin tuning in to God's wavelength, expect to enjoy abiding there. The quiet will renew you, not bore you. When words are spoken, they have more value and weight because silence is so prized.

Cautions

When you meditate and seem to hear insights, you may wonder, *Am I putting words in God's mouth? Am I making this up?* Your first line of defense is to see if it's really a committee member talking. Then check against Scripture what you believe you sensed. God doesn't say anything that's out of sync with scriptural commands (for example, to kill or exploit someone) or divine nature (God is full of integrity and mercy).

Putting Words in God's Mouth

Making up what we hear—consciously or unconsciously—usually occurs because we have an agenda in our mind. First we "hear" God say what we want to hear (at some level). For example, while meditating on the inappropriate request James and John's mother made for her sons, you decide this is a message that your mother lacks discernment and you should discount what she told you the day before. Or, if you've been studying God's grace, you immediately assume that every passage is talking about God's grace. It may be—but wait and let God speak to you rather than reading in preconceived notions.

Or we read into the text ideas that others have expressed. For example, your bossy friend keeps telling you to be more patient, so you "hear" that message in every Bible narrative. Yes, it's good to be patient, but perhaps God has something else to say to you today. If you are utterly surprised by it, that's a good sign it's from God.

When we put words in God's mouth, we replace an encounter with the living, productive, penetrating Word of God with our own ideas. If you are normally sharp and quick-thinking in Bible study, this may be especially challenging for you. You may be anxious to pour out your thoughts before they're fully baked in the oven of silence. Better to sit with them and let the yeast of the Holy Spirit take full effect.

If you think you might be controlling the meditation, ask yourself, *Am I writing the script or receiving it? Am I able to be surprised by what comes to me?* It can be difficult to surrender the control to God, but it's worth it because you will hear what you really need to know in life. You may even be afraid to hear what God would say to you, but try it. It's an exciting adventure into real interaction with God, and, as Thelma Hall wrote, "we will never be 'in charge' in prayer if it is real."[8]

If you find yourself forcing something artificial, admit it and set it aside. Then ask God, "What else?" If nothing else comes, hold on to the original idea, but wait. You will know the authenticity of it by its fruit, by what it leads you to do (see Matthew 7:20). You can also test its authenticity by running it by someone wiser than you in the Lord—a mentor or spiritual director. Or you may wish to journal about it and read it later to test it yourself. Don't be discouraged by this process; it is good training in learning to hear the Shepherd's voice (see John 10:3-4).

If you continually come up with clever insights that are probably yours, work at grounding yourself in the details of the setting and culture of the passage. Focus on the kind of work shepherds did and what the grasslands Jacob slept on would have looked like. Details will immerse you in the text, keep you focused, and help you let go of your agenda. (You may wish to invest in books that immerse you in the culture of Bible times. As you do the exercises in this book, notice each chapter's endnotes to figure out which books might help you most in this. Alfred Edersheim's *The Life and Times of Jesus the Messiah* is one particularly good reference.)

Looking for Pixie Dust

In the beginning, times of meditation are likely to be uneven. One day, words and scenes may jump out at you, but the next day the passage seems about as engaging as the telephone book. It may seem as though nothing happens. Don't let this worry you. Remember that the goal is to seek God only, not tingly experiences. Even small insights move you along. You don't need fireworks every time.

Bonhoeffer wrote that overeagerness to discover new insights in meditation

> diverts us and feeds our vanity. It is sufficient if the Word, as we read and understand it, penetrates and dwells within us. It strives to stir us, to work and operate in us, so that we shall not get away from it the whole day long. Then it will do its work in us, often without our being conscious of it. "Seek God, not happiness"—this is the fundamental rule of all meditation. If you seek God alone, you will gain happiness: That is his promise.[9]

Another way of treating meditation like pixie dust is viewing it as a problem-solving technique. God does want to solve your problems, but meditation will play a part as your perceptions change: of who God is, of who you are, and of how God wants to use you. Our goal is to seek God. That's it. Then "all these things will be given to you as well" (Matthew 6:33).

So if you've sworn off seeking pixie dust, what do you do if nothing seems to happen in your meditation? Meditation is not something you can control. Let God be in charge. You have not wasted time. You're connecting with God and training yourself to let God speak to you. Taste what it means to "abide" in God (John 15:4-10, NRSV).

THINKING NEGATIVELY

Meditation can be very helpful or very fearful for those suffering from depression or plagued by negative thinking patterns. It can be fearful if we latch onto negative ideas and find the worst-case scenario in every passage. For instance, you might meditate on the story of the prodigal son and never get past the word *squandered,* which appears only in the third verse of the passage (see Luke 15:13). This prevents you from hearing the great hope Jesus filled this parable with.

That doesn't mean you shouldn't meditate if you are depressed or prone to negativity. Meditation can be a powerful tool in building core truths lacking in your soul: you are loved by God no matter what; you are worthwhile in God's eyes; God can transform lives and personalities; God can use you to love others and pull them back from their slide into sin and despair. These healing, redemptive themes can help your reality become aligned with the reality of who God is and how God relates to you.

So if you get stuck in a negative whirlpool in the midst of meditating, ask, What is the next step? After the boy squandered his life, then what? It's also helpful to meditate with someone else in case you need to work through why you become stuck on certain words.

Questions and Activities for Individual Reflection or Group Discussion

1. What, if anything, was said in this chapter that has made you think?

2. As you prepare to meditate, what would work best for you regarding one of these details?

> *keeping pen and paper nearby*
> *choosing a time of day*
> *choosing the Scripture text*

3. Which of these committee members interfere with your thoughts?

    looking-good kid   *attitude police*
    kickback kid   *grouch*
    rescuer   *other*

4. In the next chapter, we're going to study a common method of meditation, *lectio divina*. To prepare, let's walk through a passage and approach it meditatively. Follow these directions:

Group leader instructions for question 4: Choose one group member to be the leader. The leader will slowly and quietly read instructions 1–10 aloud, pausing as directed. Pause after each instruction for a few minutes—at least two or three, and more if the group prefers it.

Also choose two readers. One will read the passage thoughtfully as directed in step 2. The other will read it slowly and thoughtfully as directed in step 6.

For this exercise, group members do not answer questions aloud. They simply listen to the questions and ponder them. If they wish, they can write their thoughts on paper. It may be frustrating for some not to discuss aloud, but it's also enriching to experience the fellowship that occurs while being quiet together.

After group members are finished with step 10, the leader can invite them to share their responses to the question in step 9: "What is this passage calling me to do?" This is not a time for group members to evaluate the time of meditation but to tell other members what they believe God was saying to them. Do not push this. Some may have found that what they believe they heard is too obscure or too personal to share comfortably. Encourage all to read the passage again before going to bed tonight.

God Rescues Us and Delights in Us: Psalm 18:4-19

1. Quiet yourself by relaxing and breathing in and out several times. Ask the Holy Spirit to speak to you through the words of this passage. Take a minute or two to do this.

2. Thoughtfully read the passage of Scripture aloud.

DEEP TROUBLE

The cords of death entangled me; the torrents of destruction overwhelmed me. The cords of the grave coiled around me; the snares of death confronted me. In my distress I called to the LORD; I cried to my God for help.

GOD HEARS

From his temple he heard my voice; my cry came before him, into his ears. The earth trembled and quaked, and the foundations of the mountains shook; they trembled because he was angry. Smoke rose from his nostrils; consuming fire came from his mouth, burning coals blazed out of it.

GOD RESCUES

*He parted the heavens and came down; dark clouds were under his
feet. He mounted the cherubim and flew; he soared on the wings of
the wind. He made darkness his covering, his canopy around him—
the dark rain clouds of the sky. Out of the brightness of his presence
clouds advanced, with hailstones and bolts of lightning. The LORD
thundered from heaven; the voice of the Most High resounded. He
shot his arrows and scattered the enemies, great bolts of lightning and
routed them. The valleys of the sea were exposed and the foundations
of the earth laid bare at your rebuke, O LORD, at the blast of breath
from your nostrils.*

*He reached down from on high and took hold of me; he drew me
out of deep waters. He rescued me from my powerful enemy, from
my foes, who were too strong for me. They confronted me in the day
of my disaster, but the LORD was my support. He brought me out
into a spacious place; he rescued me because he delighted in me.*

3. Study the passage for a few moments by considering the following
    historical background on David's experiences: David sang this
    psalm to the Lord "when the LORD delivered him from the hand of
    all his enemies and from the hand of Saul." Read the following
    background facts about David fleeing Saul and put yourself in
    David's place. After you've read the list, think of a few words that
    describe how you would have felt if you were David. [Ask group
    members to read the bulleted items silently and then pause.]

    • *Saul repeatedly tried to kill David even though David was his son-
      in-law, the best friend of his son, and the captain of his bodyguard
      (see 1 Samuel 22:14).*

- *To escape from Saul, David fled to deserts, lived in caves, and stayed with foreign kings.*

- *The first time Saul tried to kill David, David was playing the harp to soothe Saul, and Saul hurled a spear at him (see 18:10-11).*

- *One time David had to escape from Saul through a window (see 19:11-12).*

- *In a desperate attempt to escape from Saul, David stayed with Achish king of Gath, where he pretended to be insane to ensure his safety. To keep up the game, he made marks on the doors of the gate and let saliva run down his beard (see 21:10-15).*

- *When Ahimelech the priest inquired of the Lord for David, Saul killed him as well as eighty-five other priests (see 22:9-18).*

- *After David saved the city of Keilah, he had to flee because the people of Keilah were going to surrender him to Saul (see 23:5-13).*

- *David spared Saul's life several times (see 24:1-15).*

4. Place yourself in the passage with these questions: David said that God rescued him "because he delighted in me" (Psalm 18:19). Have you ever felt that God delighted in you? If so, when? If not, what would a person have to do to get God to delight in him or her?

5. Picture the activity in this passage by (a) imagining God parting the heavens, mounting the cherubim, and soaring. Don't worry about getting a precise picture of God—just picture all that activity. (Doesn't it remind you of a John Wayne saga or a *Star Wars* movie?); and (b) picturing the objects, creatures, and actions in the passage. If there are too many, choose a few.

6. With this preparation, read the passage aloud again. Read very slowly this time, imagining the actions and objects.

7. Sit for a few minutes with your eyes closed. Recall the activities in the passage. Do any of them stand out to you?

8. Sit for a few more minutes with your eyes closed. Ask God this question: "What do I need to know from this passage?"

9. Ask yourself, *What is this passage calling me to do?* Don't try to come up with something. Wait and see what comes to you.

10. Pray in response to this passage. For example, you can tell God how you feel about what you sensed from this passage. You can thank God for times of rescue. You can ask God to show you how to live in the security that God always sees you and helps you when you need it.

Chapter Six

TASTING THE WORDS OF SCRIPTURE

THE ANCIENT ART OF LECTIO DIVINA

You probably learned to study the Bible by using methods that others taught you. Perhaps you studied with a leader or teacher or a study book. We can do the same with meditation, using methods that experienced Christians have found helpful for centuries. Yet none of these methods are legalisms. We can innovate as needed.

As stated earlier, one of the oldest and most common methods of meditation is *lectio divina,* a Latin phrase meaning "divine reading" or "sacred reading." Based on the idea of "lay[ing] hold" and "keeping" (Proverbs 4:3-4), *lectio* has been used by individuals and groups for centuries. Its practice has varied, but the approach is the same: "that God's word is a 'good' word, that it benefits the reader, providing nurture, comfort, and refreshment. *Lectio* is an encounter with the living God; it is prayer."[1]

Lectio divina usually includes four phases:

1. reading the Scripture
2. meditating on the Scripture

3. praying the Scripture

4. contemplating the Scripture

Here is a closer look at these parts.

1. READING THE SCRIPTURE (*Lectio*)

It helps to read the Scripture passage aloud twice. Reading aloud slowly and respectfully helps our ears truly hear the words and phrases and creates a sense of the Lord speaking directly to us. This breaks up the familiar singsong way we sometimes hear Scripture. Reading it aloud twice penetrates those zoned-out thoughts: *uh huh . . . I know this . . . oh yeah . . .* and causes words and phrases to stand out. After you're practiced in *lectio,* you may not need to read the passage aloud if you're doing it privately.

Before reading, it's helpful to remind ourselves that Scripture is Spirit-breathed and to say to ourselves: *I am filled with the Holy Spirit. I am well equipped to hear God today.* This reminds us to set aside our previous agenda on the passage. In openness to God we ask, *What is it I don't understand or comprehend or believe in my heart of hearts today that I need to absorb more fully?* Asking such questions makes us the kind of people about whom others wonder, *Why does he get so much out of the Bible and I don't? Why does she get such terrific insights from the Word and I don't?* You've known people like that. It's because of their openness.

2. MEDITATING ON THE SCRIPTURE (*Meditatio*)

We enter into the text, prayerfully pondering the words, relishing them and cherishing them because we are open to the possibility of drawing personal meaning from them. We listen even after the reading is over to sense what words resonate in our ears or shimmer in our memory.

As thoughts come, we respond with a childlike inquisitiveness, wondering:

- *How is my life touched today by this passage?*
- *What is this passage inviting me to do?*
- *How do I feel about what is being said?*
  Why do I feel that way?
- *How do I respond deep within? Why am I*
  responding in this manner?

If no flashes of insight come, do not be concerned. That's not unusual, and insights should not be forced. If insights do come, probe them. Francis de Sales said of meditation: "Imitate the bees, who do not leave a flower as long as they can extract any honey out of it."[2]

3. PRAYING THE SCRIPTURE (*Oratio*)

Based on what we read in the passage and what we sense, we respond to God. *Lectio divina* is a dialogue: God speaks to us; we respond to God. We might pray a simple prayer, such as "Show me how . . . ," "Thank you for . . . ," or "Help me . . . " Or we can pray back the words of the passage. Here are some examples (nonitalicized words are from Scripture):

Forgive me for the times I have wanted to stop *someone* because
he was not one of us. *I confess that I have not realized that* whoever is not against us is for us. *Help me to honor* anyone who
gives . . . a cup of water in [your] name. *(Mark 9:38-41)*
O God, *it is you who has* measured the waters in the hollow of
your hand, or with the breadth of your hand marked off the

heavens. *You have* held the dust of the earth in a basket, *and* weighed the mountains on the scales and the hills in a balance. *(Isaiah 40:12)*

O *Lord, you are* gracious and compassionate, slow to anger and rich in love. *You are* good to all; *you have* compassion on all *you have* made. *You are* faithful to all *your* promises and loving toward all *you have* made. *You uphold* all those who fall and *lift* up all who are bowed down *(Psalm 145:8-9, 13-14, emphasizing the six times the word all occurs).*

4. CONTEMPLATING THE SCRIPTURE (*Contemplatio*)

Contemplation is resting in God. We don't ask questions as we do in meditation. Words become less important than fellowship with God. We bask in the deep security that our names are engraved on the palm of God's hand so that we are never forgotten and we're always in the forefront of God's mind (see Isaiah 49:16).

So instead of actively pondering, contemplation involves waiting on God in silence. This is not a negative, tiresome waiting, but one full of alertness, hope, and expectancy (see Psalm 33:18-22; 130:5-7). Waiting seems like a waste of time in a production-oriented culture, but it's actually a time to listen and to open our minds and hearts to whatever God might want to communicate. Sometimes the dots don't immediately connect between the Scripture we read (or the words that stand out) and the events of our life, but they often do begin to connect as we wait on God. Contemplation helps "to coalesce the experience of the previous three steps. In this time of quiet one is open to the inspirations of the Holy Spirit which may come by way of new insights, new perceptions, or a new infusion of peace, joy, and love."[3]

Contemplation is not dry or fretful. Contemplation is about love. According to John of the Cross, a sixteenth-century monk, "Contemplation is nothing else than a secret and peaceful and loving inflow of God, which, if not hampered, fires the soul in the spirit of love."[4]

Does contemplation sound too mystical or unusual to you? If so, don't close your eyes during contemplation. Instead open them and set a piece of paper before you. Doodle or draw in the margins. Continue to focus on what the passage is inviting you to do and see what comes to you. This too is a form of contemplation, perhaps easier for you.

Lectio PRINCIPLES UNDERGIRD MEDITATION

As we try other methods of meditation, the basic principles of lectio carry over. For example, in *lectio,* meditation occurs within the bookends of prayer. You pray at the beginning for awareness of the presence of God and you respond in prayer. You train yourself never to walk away from Scripture without responding.

Like all meditation, *lectio* doesn't bypass the mind. The mind becomes an active partner in Bible reading, which retrains it to be fixed on God. Meditation then engages the whole person: body and soul, mind and heart, intellect and imagination, will and emotions.

Lectio is centered on the idea of *invitation,* as all meditation is. You invite God to speak to you. In the passage, God invites you to hear, to consider something you may not have considered before. Like the *Selah* pauses in Psalms, pauses in *lectio* let you hear God's invitations.

As you practice this type of meditation, consider that you are joining a communion of saints who for hundreds of years knew and loved God by meditating on the Word of God.

A TRUE DIALOGUE

Once I was meditating on 1 Corinthians 12 and having a difficult time because it was so familiar to me and I struggled against thinking in auto-pilot—*Yeah, yeah, everybody helps each other, we work together, yeah, yeah.* But when I read the passage aloud the second time, verse 21 startled me: "The eye cannot say to the hand, 'I don't need you!' And the head cannot say to the feet, 'I don't need you!'" To my surprise, the face of a person I couldn't stand came to me.

Taken aback, I spoke aloud to God, "But I've never told her I don't need her!" The thought came to me (one of the ways God speaks to us), *She knows it anyway.* I became upset and prayed, "Oh God, I don't want to need her. She's been so cruel to me and my family. It's true! I don't need her around."

I hadn't thought of this person for months, but the memory of her surfaced while meditating on Scripture. I can't explain this any other way but that the Holy Spirit brought her to my mind.

I was at the point in *lectio* where it was time to pray, so I took this next step: *Show me this woman's heart.* As I sat in silence waiting on God, I remembered her showing me childhood pictures of herself that revealed the deep hurt she'd experienced. In response to this input from God, I wanted to pray for her.

But what would I pray? What did she need? Because of the dark childhood pictures I remembered, I began to pray Zephaniah 3:17: "The LORD your God is with you, he is mighty to save. He will take great delight in you, he will quiet you with his love, he will rejoice over you with singing." I pictured God singing over her, holding her, and rocking her. (I'd linked the rocking image with this verse many years earlier because I used to sing to my kids when I rocked them as babies.)

As I moved to the next step of contemplation and resting in God, I did not experience quietness and peace. Nagging thoughts needed to be addressed. I sensed God asking me a question I have so often asked when I've led support groups: What are you going to do about what I showed you?

I was disturbed. Picturing this woman in God's arms and praying for her had been a difficult enough struggle. I wasn't willing to do anything more. So I sat there. I would not—could not—force myself to make plans to be chummy with her. I waited. In the years before I'd begun meditating, I would have forced myself at this point to resolve to call her on the telephone even though I didn't want to, and I would have done it with the wrong heart. Meditating had taught me not to coerce myself to do something *I* thought I should do but to let *God* lead me into being willing to do something that seemed to come to me from God. Waiting on God also helps us acknowledge that God has better ideas than we do, and God will tell us what they are.

As I waited and sat in the quiet, I tried to be completely open to God. I soon recalled how during the greeting time at church, I habitually moved toward people who sat opposite where she sat. Gulp. I sensed God inviting me to go out of my way to greet her. I confessed to God that I did not want to do this. I waited some more.

By this time I was so overwrought that I was lying with my face on the floor. In the quiet the Holy Spirit gave me the nerve to make this proposal to God: "If you give me the grace, I will step out to greet her—*every other* week, not every week. Give me the grace to do this."

Such back and forth negotiations with God tell us that meditation is not always a warm, fuzzy encounter. It can be edgy. The one who loves us also confronts us (see, for example, Mark 10:21).

This story illustrates the helpfulness of following the framework of *lectio divina.* I was uncomfortable during most of the process, but the steps of reading, meditating, praying, and contemplating moved me forward into hearing what I needed to hear and doing what God was leading me to do. This keeps us from simply reading a passage, experiencing thoughts and feelings, and walking away. We need to respond to God in prayer and then let God have the last word in contemplation.

This story also illustrates how connecting inwardly with God changes outward behavior. As a result of this time of *lectio divina,* I greeted this woman every few weeks. But I didn't feel resentful toward God about doing it. I knew I was being stretched and I tried to cooperate with what I believed God had invited me in secret to do. My greetings surprised her, and after several other events occurred (which I did not engineer), we became friends again.

Compare this scenario with ones in which someone tries to persuade you to apologize to someone you're at odds with. In the long run, that method does not work unless your heart becomes aligned with God's. In meditation God comes alongside you, looks at you, loves you, and challenges you to move forward—usually in some simple, doable way. Eventually, you find that because God loves you, you'll do anything God asks.

"CERTAIN USEFUL INSTRUCTIONS"

If the four steps of *lectio* seem too vague to you, understand that meditation is more about attitude and approach than mechanics. Some detailed exercises follow, but first let's hear from the wise Francis de Sales writing in *Introduction to the Devout Life,* as he offered "certain useful instructions" about how to do *lectio divina.*

PREPARE BY BECOMING AWARE OF THE PRESENCE OF GOD

To be more conscious of God's presence, you might pray the Lord's Prayer or sing a hymn or chorus. Or you can say a verse from Psalms about God's presence: "You have made known to me the path of life; you will fill me with joy in your presence, with eternal pleasures at your right hand" (Psalm 16:11; or see Psalm 139:1-10).

> *Whenever you have moments of study and meditation, [remember] God is always present with you—that is God's omnipotent nature and the Son who is with you always and the Spirit who doesn't forsake us—but we are not always conscious of it.*[5]

LET YOUR MEDITATION AFFECT YOUR WILL AND EMOTIONS

Too often Bible reading is an intellectual activity only. Besides stimulating our thinking, meditation moves "the will, the affective part of our soul, [to] *love* of God and neighbor, *desire* for heaven and glory, *zeal* for the salvation of souls, *imitation* of the life of our Lord, *confidence* in God's goodness and mercy, and deep *sorrow* for the sins of our past life,"[6] according to Francis de Sales. The will chooses feelings such as desire, confidence, and sorrow.

De Sales also urged us to let our times of meditation move even further to prayerful planning for action (resolutions).[7] We don't just relish our deep insights; we also advance from *knowing* what is right to *wanting* to do what is right to *prayerfully planning* how we might do it. In other words we ask ourselves, *What am I going to do about this insight I've received?*

The outcome of such prayerful planning cannot be altogether forced. For example, when we sense God urging us to let go of bitterness toward someone, too often we pressure ourselves to say or do something sweet toward that person. Or we try to conjure up amiable feelings. What is missing is a change of heart. We need to ask God to put within us longing and desire to love those who have wronged us and to believe that whatever happened to us can be redeemed. Meditation creates a climate in which this change of heart is likely to occur because we are in the midst of a personal encounter with God.

Meditation devoid of resolutions can be dangerous, De Sales warned: "Remember the decisions you have made and carefully put them into effect on that very day. Without it meditation is often not only useless but even harmful. Virtues meditated on but not practiced sometimes inflate our minds and courage and we think that we are really such as we have thought and resolved to be."[8] We fool ourselves into thinking we are more holy than we are—just because we thought holy thoughts for a minute or two.

To remind myself of decisions made during meditation, I often leave my Bible open to the passage all day and set it on my desk, bed, or dining room table. Whenever I see that open Bible, I remember how God spoke to me and I am more likely to move forward.

In making resolutions, we need to ask God to show us what is reasonable and doable, given our character. In my dialogue with God about 1 Corinthians 12, I knew that greeting the woman I disliked every week was not possible for me. To greet her at all seemed impossible. So I made it more doable by aiming for every other week. Such strategizing follows the advice of the early-twentieth-century Benedictine Dom Chapman's: "Pray as you can, not as you can't."[9] We spend far too much time beating ourselves up for what we are unwilling or unable to do, instead of taking the next step and doing what we can do.

This "pray as you can" principle crosses over to other disciplines and activities: love as you can, not as you can't; serve as you can, not as you can't; even meditate as you can, not as you can't. Focus on what you can do, and do it. And keep doing what you can do. If you focus on what you can't do, your sense of inadequacy distracts you and your spirituality becomes about you. By doing what you can do (with the help of the Holy Spirit), you keep your spirituality focused on God.

MEDITATE ON PASSAGES OF TEN VERSES OR LESS

As mentioned earlier, the culture of modernity prods us to finish reading a page, a section, or a chapter. Bonhoeffer counseled, "It is not necessary that we should get through the entire passage in one meditation. Often we shall have to stop with one sentence or even one word, because we have been gripped and arrested and cannot evade it any longer."[10] Limiting the words to meditate on retrains us away from that rushed feeling of having to finish the selection for the day. Finishing something is not the point. The point is to hear God.

Perhaps you regularly study larger portions of Scripture in school or a Bible study, or you're following a yearly Bible reading program. That's too much to meditate on. If this is true, when you read or study make a note of ten-verse portions that you would like to come back to for times of meditation.

DOING *Lectio Divina* IN A GROUP

Group *lectio* combines several spiritual disciplines. It involves meditation on Scripture, but it is also the practice of community. Many people understand fellowship or community to be only about talking or discussing or eating together. While it may include those activities, community also involves listening and being quiet together. In *Making All Things New*, Henri Nouwen, once a professor at the University of

Notre Dame, Yale, and Harvard, wrote:

> *In our wordy world we usually spend our time together talking. We
> feel most comfortable in sharing experiences, discussing interesting
> subjects, or arguing about current issues. It is through a very active
> verbal exchange that we try to discover each other. But often we find
> that words function more as walls than as gates, more as ways to keep
> distance than to come close. Often—even against our own desires—
> we find ourselves competing with each other. We try to prove to each
> other that we are worth being paid attention to, that we have some-
> thing to show that makes us special.*
>
> > *The discipline of community helps us to be silent together. This
> disciplined silence is not an embarrassing silence, but a silence in
> which together we pay attention to the Lord who calls us together. In
> this way we come to know each other not as people who cling anx-
> iously to our self-constructed identity, but as people who are loved by
> the same God in a very intimate and unique way.*[11]

Being quiet together is a different kind of fellowship that may take
some people a while to get used to. But it deepens the eventual discussion. For example, Quaker "spiritual friendship" groups incorporate
silence with sharing. Some of these groups begin with thirty minutes of
silence, then each person talks.[12] Beginning with a time of silence
changes the way we are with people. We learn to truly listen to them
without thinking about what we want to say next or without thinking
of how we react to what they say. Wrote Bonhoeffer, "Christians have
forgotten that the ministry of listening has been committed to them by
Him who is Himself the great listener and whose work they should
share."[13] Instead of jabbering, we learn to be truly present to each other.

Imagine for a moment a church meeting in which people of various opinions have become frustrated with each other. What if they took a breather and did a *lectio divina* exercise together? Just the act of calming themselves could transform the tone of the meeting. After encountering God in Scripture, people would no doubt speak to each other differently and leave the meeting still loving each other.

During one such meeting, I wanted to do this but I couldn't because I wasn't in charge. So while a vote was taken, I went to the piano and began playing "The Old Rugged Cross." I moved from hymn to hymn until the voting was done. Several of us behaved with much more calmness and civility after that.

Lectio resembles a Bible study group because participants pray for each other and answer questions aloud. But it differs because people are also quiet together, any talk is quiet and unhurried, and participants use as few words as possible. An advantage of doing *lectio* in a group is that it may help participants stay focused because others around them are focused. (Detailed instructions for how to do group *lectio* are given in appendix A.)

Questions and Activities for Individual Reflection or Group Discussion

1. What, if anything, was said in this chapter that has made you think?

2. If you were locked up in a prison camp, what words or phrases in Scripture that you've been able to "keep" and "lay hold of" would mean the most to you? (Don't worry about quoting Scripture verses exactly right.)

3. Which of these quotations is most helpful to you? Why?

> "Pray as you can, not as you can't." —*Dom Chapman*
> "In [being silent together], we come to know each other not as people who cling anxiously to our self-constructed identity, but as people

who are loved by the same God in a very intimate and unique way."—Henri Nouwen
"Christians have forgotten that the ministry of listening has been committed to them by Him who is Himself the great listener and whose work they should share."—Dietrich Bonhoeffer

4. Try the following *lectio divina* exercise. If doing this meditation alone, read the Scripture aloud. To answer questions, you may simply think about them or wish to write responses. Ignore instructions to the group leader. This exercise and others in this book include helps for those who are prone to read the Scripture in sleep mode. I confess that I developed the bad habit of zoning out when Scripture was read, as if the reader had begun with, "Once upon a time . . ." I've provided optional activities with the meditation exercises to help you concentrate on the words after the passage is read. Some or all of the following are included to prod you to truly enter into the passage after reading it. You may skip these if you wish.

> *Study Options—I've italicized certain words in the Scripture reading and highlighted them again in the Study Options section. This section explains words that are not easily understood, provides historical or cultural or biographical background for the passage, or offers distances and visual cues that make it easier to imagine the scene or the feelings of the characters.*
>
> *Pondering Options—These questions are designed to help you put yourself in the place of the characters or ponder the meanings of phrases or concepts in the passage. Using them will train you to get inside a passage in order to meditate on it and to turn over ideas behind the words.*
>
> *Cues for Picturing the Passage—When imagining the situation*

described in Scripture, you may need cues about how the setting looked or how the culture of that day affected what happened. This option often includes suggested scenes to picture.

Group leader instructions for question 4: Read the previous individual instructions. In each section of the meditation exercise, there are instructions for the group leader. The leader should review these ahead of time to be ready to lead the group. Before beginning, the group leader should read the three previous paragraphs to understand the helps that are included. Move through the exercise, noting when participants are finished reading or praying, and then continuing on.

Choosing Not to Judge Others: Luke 6:37-45

QUIETING YOURSELF

Center yourself by breathing in and out several times. Bend your neck back and forth and let your muscles relax. Offer each distracting thought to God. Try using the "palms down, palms up" method described in chapter 4.

Optional warm-up prayer—If you're having trouble settling down, offer this prayer: "Give me the ability to see good things in unexpected places, and talents in unexpected people. And give me, O Lord, the grace to tell them so."[14]

1. READING THE SCRIPTURE (*Lectio*)

Ask the Holy Spirit to speak to you through the words of the following Bible passage, and then read it aloud. If the story is familiar to you, set aside what you know about it and read each word with fresh eyes.

TREATING PEOPLE WITH GENEROSITY

"Do not judge, and you will not be judged. Do not condemn, and you will not be condemned. Forgive, and you will be forgiven. Give, and it will be given to you. A good measure, pressed down, shaken together and running over, will be poured into your lap. For with the measure you use, it will be measured to you."

CHOOSING HEROES CAREFULLY

He also told them this parable: "Can a blind man lead a blind man? Will they not both fall into a pit? A student is not above his teacher, but everyone who is fully trained will be like his teacher."

LACK OF CREDENTIALS TO JUDGE

"Why do you look at the speck of sawdust in your brother's eye and pay no attention to the plank in your own eye? How can you say to

your brother, 'Brother, let me take the speck out of your eye,' when you yourself fail to see the plank in your own eye? You hypocrite, first take the plank out of your eye, and then you will see clearly to remove the speck from your brother's eye."

INNER THOUGHTS COUNT

"No good tree bears bad fruit, nor does a bad tree bear good fruit. Each tree is recognized by its own fruit. People do not pick figs from thornbushes, or grapes from briers. The good man brings good things out of the good stored up in his heart, and the evil man brings evil things out of the evil stored up in his heart. For out of the overflow of his heart his mouth speaks."

Instructions for group leader for *lectio*: Pray aloud for the Holy Spirit's leading. Suggest that group members close their eyes and listen as you read the Scripture (fifteen to twenty minutes, depending on options chosen below.)

Study Options

If you want to study this passage to understand it better, review the italicized words and phrases below.

judge—The original Greek word used here means to act as a judge of someone else. This involves passing judgment and condemnation, but it is not the same thing as discerning, examining, or questioning—these are appropriate thoughts.

Can a blind man lead—Blindness was mentioned thirty-four times in the Gospels and was a common ailment because of uncovered garbage and toilets. Flies were abundant and spread diseases. Medicines were crude.

speck of sawdust in your brother's eye—It's not that we ignore wrongdoing, but we choose not to focus on others' wrongs.

hypocrite—not simply someone who says one thing and does another, but someone who doesn't even have a heart to do the right thing.

Instructions for group leader for Study Options: Wait a few minutes after reading the passage, then suggest participants silently read all the study options. When they're finished reading, continue.

Pondering Options

Use one or two of the following questions to prod your thinking about how Jesus switched the focus in life.

1. "A good measure, pressed down, shaken together and running over" presents the image of a merchant measuring grain and making sure buyers get the full amount of grain or flour they ordered. The merchant deals fairly by pressing down the grain and shaking the cup so no air pockets remain underneath—and is even generous, filling it until it runs over. Ponder the kind of heart a merchant needs to measure so fairly and generously.

2. The first three paragraphs are about how we should treat other people. (The words *you* and *your* appear nineteen times.) It's as if there's a mysterious link between how we treat others and how they

treat us. This is called reciprocity—what goes around comes around. Our worst selves, however, do not believe in reciprocity; we think we deserve special treatment. Even though I judge you harshly, I want you to judge me fairly. I want you to understand me. Reflect on an area of life in which you might experiment with reciprocity: work, family, friendship, neighborhood, people in this group or some other group.

3. Some might say these passages contradict each other. We're not to judge (see Luke 6:37), but we are to evaluate leaders carefully enough to avoid following someone we believe is blind (see verses 39-40). Consider that we can be discerning without being judgmental. Discernment looks for facts, while judging condemns. Discernment allows that I may be mistaken but judgment assumes I have superior wisdom or am morally superior. Consider what sort of heart a person needs to have in order to be discerning instead of judgmental.

4. If a good tree automatically bears good fruit, then when we are inclining our heart to God, we're more likely to behave with goodness. But an evil heart results in evil behavior. That's why it's useless to try to change an attitude or outward behavior only. Actions and attitudes flow from the heart. Consider now a troublesome situation in which your actions seem to take over and you behave in ways that are inappropriate (responding to a friend, family member, or attractive member of the opposite sex). What is probably in your heart at that moment? What do you need to have already stored in your heart in order for you to behave appropriately?

Instructions for group leader for Pondering Options: Ask participants to read the pondering options silently, choose one option, and tell their answer in *one sentence or two*. When members are finished, continue. Explain that this is not a time for discussion but for reporting brief responses to the questions. Group members may pass, if they wish.

Cues for Picturing the Passage

Before reading the passage again, consider these cues.

Character cue: Jesus as a teacher—Even though you have heard the words of this passage many times, try to imagine how Jesus' first listeners felt. They probably laughed hard at Jesus' word picture of a plank hanging out of someone's eye. Even worse, this visually handicapped person wanted to do minor eye surgery on someone else. "Stop him, quickly!" they may have howled.

How clever of Jesus to speak to us who are so deep in a moral wilderness, justifying ourselves for all kinds of harsh and judgmental behavior. Enter Jesus with funny word pictures, showing us who we are. What a gentle way to jolt our conscience.

Geographical cue: The "Mount"—The accepted location of the Sermon on the Mount is a hilly region called the Horns of Hattin in Galilee. This mountain has twin peaks with a craterlike formation in the middle.[15] Galileans, so far away from Jerusalem, weren't known for dotting each *i* and crossing each *t* in regard to the law, so they were probably eating up Jesus' teaching, which would sound unconventional to the Pharisees over in Judea.[16] In this remote setting with a huge crowd of people, it might have been easier for what Christ said to hit home.

> **Instructions for group leader for Cues for Picturing the Passage:** Have members read the cues silently. When they're finished reading, continue.

2. Meditating on the Scripture (*Meditatio*)

Reflect on how your life is touched by this passage today. Read the passage aloud again and ponder the following question for several minutes: *What word or phrase emerges from the passage and stays with you?*

Reflect a while longer and consider: *Is God offering me an invitation in this passage to enlarge my understanding or to do something in the next few days? What might that be?*

> **Instructions for group leader for meditatio:** Have another group member read the passage aloud and then state the first question printed in italics above. Have the group sit together quietly for three minutes or more and then ask group members to say quietly the word or phrase or scene that resonates for them.
>
> Wait at least five minutes and then ask the second and third questions in italics. Ask group members to respond by quietly saying, "I sense this passage calling me to . . ." and completing that statement with a short phrase. They may wish to speak with their eyes closed if this helps them remain focused.

3. Praying the Scripture (*Oratio*)

Read the passage aloud again. Pray, perhaps using one of these suggestions:

- *Tell God how you feel about what you sensed (or didn't sense).*
- *Tell God what you most want to say at this time: "Show me how . . ." or "Thank you for . . ."*

Instructions for group leader for *oratio*: Have another member of the group read the passage aloud. Invite members to pray silently, perhaps using the previous prayer suggestions.

After a few minutes, ask group members to pray for the person on their left, specifically about what the person has sensed from God. Have group members move around the circle to the right (so they'll hear clearly what is prayed for them without thinking about what they need to pray). Anyone wishing to pray silently may do so, saying, "I'm praying silently." When they're finished, they can say, "Amen."

---

4. CONTEMPLATING THE SCRIPTURE (*Contemplatio*)

Optional—Read the passage aloud again.

Take a few minutes to sit in silence and enjoy God's presence. You may wish to focus on a favorite image, such as God singing over you (see Zephaniah 3:17). If you wish, ask, "God, what is it you most want to say to me at this time?"

Instructions for group leader for *contemplatio*: If you'd like, have the passage read aloud again. Read the previous instructions and rest in a time of contemplation. Close in prayer, thanking God for speaking to members of the group (five minutes or more).

Chapter Seven

THE SANCTIFIED
IMAGINATION

USING IGNATIAN MEDITATION TO
WALK INSIDE SCRIPTURE

🌿

Imagine you are a disciple standing next to Jesus as a slick young guy walks up. In our day he would be an attractive youth minister who attends seminary and drives a Jaguar. He roars in—wow, this is the kind of guy you wish you'd been when you were twenty (if you're male) or wish you'd met (if you're female). In an act of humility, he brings himself before Jesus' face—kneeling, no less—and says, "Good teacher, what must I do to inherit eternal life?"

As a disciple standing by, you think, *What a humble guy! And he appreciates how smart Jesus is.*

But Jesus is not impressed. He quizzes the young man: "Why do you call me good? No one is good—except God alone."

You think, *If this guy describes Jesus with a word used to describe only God, he must see in Jesus the same magnificence we see.*

To answer the young man's question, Jesus says, "You know the commandments: 'Do not murder, do not commit adultery, do not steal, do not give false testimony, do not defraud, honor your father and mother.'" The capable young man replies that he has been keeping these commands since he was a boy.

This guy is so sharp, so obedient. This is getting more interesting by the minute.

But Jesus pauses. He looks at him and loves him.

What is Jesus doing? He's gazing hard at the young man—but with tenderness and warmth. What is Jesus going to say now? I bet it will be wonderful. I hope this young man becomes a follower. They say he's rich—we could use that money!

But with that intense, loving look, Jesus says, "One thing you lack. Go, sell everything you have and give to the poor, and you will have treasure in heaven."

Why does Jesus say this? Yes, Jews are commanded to help the poor and oppressed. But sell everything? We've given up everything, but we could go back to our jobs if we needed to. Can he? What's this "treasure in heaven"? That's like that time Jesus said, "For where your treasure is, there your heart will be also." So this guy's heart needs to be changed? How can that be? He's one of the sharpest guys we've met.

Then Jesus says, "Then come, follow me."

So Jesus does want him as a follower. But what about donating everything?

The man's face falls and he walks away sad.

He looks crushed. He's walking away. But Jesus loved him! Why did Jesus have to insist he give away his money? Maybe I should run after him.

The first time I meditated on this scene recorded in Mark 10:17-22, I was riveted by how Jesus looked at this good young man and loved him, but then in the atmosphere of love, challenged him to sell everything he had and give it to the poor. Since then I have continually imagined Jesus looking at me and loving me, and then challenging me to give up things I cling to. Mostly, I respond as the rich young ruler did—turning away. But Jesus keeps asking. And because I now understand that God challenges me in the midst of quiet, teeming love, offering me the grace I need, now and then I relinquish that thing I cling to.

Too often when people hear God challenging them, they sense God yelling at them or heaping guilt on them. But this cannot be accurate because God is not arrogant or manipulative (see 1 Corinthians 13:5). Even when God lays difficult truth in front of us, it's always drenched in mercy. If you believed deeply that God loves you, what might you—someday—be willing to relinquish? Meditating on this passage can help us with that process of trust and relinquishment.

THE MOVIE METHOD

The previous sequence invited you to step into a scene from Scripture, which is another method of meditation. Because you relive an event in Scripture, it can be called the movie method, or picture prayer. In the sixteenth century, Ignatius of Loyola founded the Jesuit order, training his fellow monastics with *The Spiritual Exercises,* in which this style of meditation is integral. His specific instructions have helped many. First he recommended that we place ourselves in the text as a careful observer—as a "fly on the wall." If prompted by God, we become one of the characters, seeing the story unfold from that character's viewpoint. The aim is to enter the biblical narrative to more fully participate in Jesus' mind, heart, and work.

In the previous meditation I assumed the identity of one of the disciples observing the scene. In my own experiences with the passage, however, I have normally found myself in the role of the rich young ruler. We do not choose a role, however. We start out as a bystander and may stay that way. Or we may find ourselves identifying with someone in the passage and seeing the circumstances through that person's eyes.

When meditating on a passage from a certain character's viewpoint, we try to feel what people felt or think what they thought, relying on the context. (I quoted Matthew 6:21 and incorporated the itinerant lifestyle of the disciples.) It helps to update details (seminary student, Jaguar) to get a sense of how the characters might have felt. Using this method, we "allow the stories to become alive for us by entering into them with all the knowledge, experience, and imagination we possess. It is wise to ask the Spirit to guide the use of our inner resources so that through them we may hear whatever word God wishes to speak."[1]

IMAGINARY TROUBLES

Perhaps you're bothered that the Ignatian style of meditation makes use of the imagination. Here are some reasons you might give for feeling that way.

IMAGINATION IS FANTASY—WHICH IS NOT REAL

Developmental psychologist James Fowler, who has long studied how faith develops in adults, addresses this issue: "Imagination is not to be equated with fantasy or make-believe. Rather, imagination is a powerful force underlying all knowing. In faith, imagination composes comprehensive images of the *ultimate conditions of existence*."[2] These last four words are a developmental psychologist's words for *reality*—what really is and what we really believe is true (which often differs from the "right answers" we may offer in a structured Bible study setting).

Admitting and addressing what we really believe is what changes us. For example, what is reality to most people based on their actions and unguarded speech?

> *That God loves them no matter what? Or that God is fed up with them because they make the same mistakes over and over again?*

That God is the sort of being who does nothing that isn't good or right? Or that God has let one too many good folks develop cancer? That God will work to redeem evil and wicked things that happen? Or that the world is going to pieces?

Your reality may be different from what you would tell your pastor or someone at church. What you really believe is revealed by your gut feelings and the rambling thoughts that occupy your mind—even if intellectually you know they are incorrect. For example, you may know intellectually that God loves you, but you don't believe it in your heart of hearts. A person's true beliefs (image of reality) govern thoughts, feelings, choices, and behaviors. Even if you're unaware that you have something as complex as an "image of reality," you do have one and it affects everything you think or do.

How do we adjust our "image of reality" to reality as God knows it? Studying the Bible (informational reading) provides fuel for meditation (formational reading), which changes the way we see. This, in turn, changes who we are and how we behave. Why? "The eyes of your heart [have been] enlightened" to see heaven's hope and inheritance (Ephesians 1:18). Through these enlightened eyes, we can learn to "fix our eyes not on what is seen, but on what is unseen" (2 Corinthians 4:18). We can use our imagination—a part of our mind that needs to be renewed (see Romans 12:2)—"to make things more real, to bring them before [our] mind in a more forcible way," says Dallas Willard.[3] Imagination, then, becomes the handmaiden of reason.[4]

THE BIBLE DOESN'T RECOMMEND USING THE IMAGINATION

Not only did the Israelites use their imaginations to reenact the Passover, but Jesus asked listeners to use their imaginations to picture buried treasure, an unjust judge, a mugging on the Jericho road, a house built on sand, and someone fussing over a tiny gnat in his drink without realizing he'd just swallowed a camel. Jesus stimulated listeners' imaginations by using parables, images, and word pictures.

Was Isaiah whisked to the throne room of heaven or did God bring it to his imagination (see Isaiah 6:1-5)? Did the apostle John see heaven through his physical eyes or through the interior eyes of his retrained imagination (see Revelation 10:1; 15:1; 18:1; 19:11; 20:1; 21:1,2)? We don't know, but for two thousand years Christians have used their imaginations to picture John's images from the pages of Revelation.

IMAGINATION GETS US INTO TROUBLE

It's true that imagination has been a source of false prophecy and idol worship (Isaiah 65:2; Ezekiel 13:2), but, as John Mogabgab, editor of *Weavings,* asked, "What if imagination's potential for misleading us were reconfigured by the mind of Christ, which Paul claims we possess (see 1 Corinthians 2:16)? Armed with stories, images, and hopes drawn from God's history with the people of God (as Christ's mind was), imagination can become a penetrating force.[5] The problem is that we may have let our imagination go to the devil. Jesus pinpointed this when he spoke of looking at someone lustfully and committing adultery in the heart (see Matthew 5:27-28). The imagination can be hijacked by lesser forces—ever imagine strangling your boss?

But as disciples of Jesus, we have the responsibility to let our imagination be retrained for God's purposes. We ask God to retrain every part of ourselves—tongue, thoughts, heart, feet, lips, arms, and knees—so that we are transformed into Christlikeness (see 1 Peter 3:10; 2 Corinthians 10:5; James 4:8; Ephesians 6:15; Colossians 3:8; Hebrews

12:12). We're also to renew our minds, which includes our imagination (see Romans 12:2).

A retrained imagination becomes a powerful force in God's hands. For example, it equips us better to "rejoice with those who rejoice; mourn with those who mourn" (Romans 12:15). Gene Veith wrote in *Reading Between the Lines,* "Empathy, identifying with the joys and sorrows of others, is a special application of the imagination. The ability to imagine what it would be like to experience what someone else is experiencing, to project ourselves into someone else's point of view, can be crucial to moral sensitivity."[6] With the help of my imagination, I'm more likely to

> *incorporate the doctrines of Scripture into my reality,*
> *and thus have faith*
> *understand the viewpoint of the disgruntled, and thus offer hope*
> *be compassionate to the hurting, and thus show love*

So the imagination must be retrained and even nurtured. Scripture meditation is a primary tool to turn the imagination around. Oswald Chambers challenges us: "Is your imagination stayed on God or is it starved? The starvation of the imagination is one of the most fruitful sources of exhaustion and sapping in a worker's life. If you have never used your imagination to put yourself before God, begin to do it now. Imagination is the greatest gift God has given us and it ought to be devoted entirely to Him."[7]

So you have a choice: Let your imagination keep getting you into trouble or let God baptize it daily to transform your soul into Christlikeness.

I CAN'T MEDITATE BECAUSE I DON'T HAVE MUCH IMAGINATION

Can you worry? If so, then you have a rich imagination. Worry is brooding over events, turning them over and over. So is meditation—but for good. Worry is about playing out scenarios, asking, *What if this happened?* Meditation is asking, *What if I were the rich young ruler? What then?*

You can spark your imagination when reading a narrative passage by pondering, *Hmmm, I don't think I would have acted that way. Instead, I would have . . .* What if you were the father of the prodigal son and your older son was being self-righteous and mulish during the party at the end? If I had been the father, I'm sure I would have been irritated. I might have told the servants to tell the older son he could stay outside until he got his attitude straight, and then I would have had the servants lock the doors. Perhaps you would have been a whiner and cajoler and gone out there and pleaded with him. The father—so much the gentle but clear-headed God we love—uttered the most beautiful words of the parable (which is a story Christ made up with his imagination): "My son, . . . you are always with me, and everything I have is yours" (Luke 15:31). The next time you're being stubborn and self-absorbed, picture God saying those words to you. (Step-by-step instructions for meditating on this parable are included at the close of this chapter.)

THE INFORMED IMAGINATION

If you are afraid of imaginative meditation because you might distort the intended meaning of the Scripture, you have a valid concern. People distort every spiritual discipline—Bible study, prayer, fasting, and so on. That doesn't mean you ignore these disciplines, but instead you diligently learn how to meditate from those who have done it well. And if you meditate alone, use a passage you have studied so that you're familiar with the historical, linguistic, and cultural facts. That way you know who is speaking and being spoken to. If you have a sense of the history of the passage you're less likely to distort it.

Also keep meditation as word-centered as possible. Meditation isn't something you make up and drift with. It stays centered in the words of Scripture. For example, try to picture the look on Jesus' face when he said these words: "Friend, do what you came for" (Matthew 26:50).

Let's set the scene first (because study comes before meditation). Jesus is in the garden of Gethsemane. He has just prayed the prayer about letting the cup pass from him and then doing God's will. Judas has come forward with soldiers behind him to arrest Jesus. Jesus turns to Judas and says, "Friend, do what you came for." Instead of guessing what Jesus was thinking, let his words illuminate what his thoughts and emotions might have been. Shut your eyes and ponder those exact words: "Friend, do what you came for." What look do you imagine on Jesus' face based on the words he said? Pause and try it.

Responses to this usually include such things as love and compassion. This is borne out in the word *Friend*. Jesus did not say, "Jerk, do what you came for." He didn't seem to be angry. He went out of his way to address Judas as "friend."

Perhaps you also sense resignation on Jesus' part. But the tone is much stronger. The sentence is constructed in the imperative voice, which means it's a command. (The subject of the sentence is the understood *you*.) This is much more than passive relinquishment. This is determination. "*Do* what you came for." Jesus was never a victim of circumstances, unable to keep himself from being crucified. He always knew what was going to happen and acted with clear intent. This small sentence is so illustrative of the character of God: courage and gentleness; firmness and love; justice and mercy; truth and grace. Jesus knew how to speak the truth in love.

PUT YOUR WHOLE SELF INTO MEDITATION

Sometimes you may wish to reenact the scene, putting your whole body into it, taking the pose of one character. For example, in Luke 13:10-17 Jesus healed a woman "who had been crippled by a spirit for eighteen years. She was bent over and could not straighten up at all" (verse 11). In her book *Journaling: A Spirit Journey*, Anne Broyles recommends that before reading this passage, we spend three minutes walking around bent over in half: "Imagine yourself talking to people you meet on the street. How does it feel to relate to others from this stance? Can you imagine always looking down instead of up?"[8] After walking around my living room bent over for three minutes, the passage was riveting to read.

After reading the passages, Broyles recommends:

> *Think of the woman who spent eighteen years bent over in a spirit of infirmity. How was her vision narrowed? What possibilities would have been closed to her?*
>
> *How would you identify the bent-over part of yourself?*
>
> *Write a prayer to Jesus, detailing your own infirmity (weakness, failing). Share your feelings honestly, knowing you will be heard. Take a few moments of silence. Then write what Jesus might say to you, as he said to the woman bent over for eighteen years: "Woman, you are freed from your frailty."*[9]

Pause and answer one of the previous questions.

Picturing the passage requires that we become directors of the movie in our imaginations, with the Bible text as our script. A director has to figure out what everyone is doing. For example, in one of the healings Jesus "put his fingers into the man's ears. Then he spit and touched the man's tongue" (Mark 7:33). If you try to picture yourself doing what Jesus did, how would you have to position yourself in front of the man? When I tried to do this, I saw myself cradling the man's jaw. Imagine having Jesus cradle your jaw and feeling the vibration from within Jesus as he sighs deeply and cries out, "'Ephphatha!' (which means, 'Be opened!')" (verse 35). How would it feel to be that deaf man? Then consider what it would be like to hear your own voice for the first time.

Use All Five Senses During Meditation

One of the key features of Ignatian meditation is experiencing a passage with all five senses. If I had been a participant in this scene, what would I have seen? Heard? Touched? Smelled? Tasted? According to the authors of *Prayer and Temperament*, "We should try to imagine not only what we would see but also what the wood of the cross would feel like, the smell of the sheep, and the taste of the sour wine given to Jesus. The purpose behind the insistence of St. Ignatius on this vivid recall of past events is to try to make the event as real as possible."[10]

Let's walk through the scene in Luke 8:26-39, noting how we can enter into it with our senses. Be alert for the four senses the details of this particular text call into action. First quiet yourself for a moment and then read the passage aloud.

"Before"

They sailed to the region of the Gerasenes, which is across the lake from Galilee. When Jesus stepped ashore, he was met by a demon-possessed man from the town. For a long time this man had not worn clothes or lived in a house, but had lived in the tombs. When he saw

Jesus, he cried out and fell at his feet, shouting at the top of his voice,
"What do you want with me, Jesus, Son of the Most High God? I
beg you, don't torture me!" For Jesus had commanded the evil spirit to
come out of the man. Many times it had seized him, and though he
was chained hand and foot and kept under guard, he had broken his
chains and had been driven by the demon into solitary places.
[Compare "No one was strong enough to subdue him. Night and day
among the tombs and in the hills he would cry out and cut himself
with stones" (Mark 5:4-5).]

THE DRAMATIC RESCUE

Jesus asked him, "What is your name?"
"Legion," he replied, because many demons had gone into him.
And they begged him repeatedly not to order them to go into the
Abyss.
A large herd of pigs was feeding there on the hillside. The
demons begged Jesus to let them go into them, and he gave them per-
mission. When the demons came out of the man, they went into the
pigs, and the herd rushed down the steep bank into the lake and was
drowned.
When those tending the pigs saw what had happened, they ran
off and reported this in the town and countryside, and the people
went out to see what had happened.

"AFTER"

When they came to Jesus, they found the man from whom the
demons had gone out, sitting at Jesus' feet, dressed and in his right
mind; and they were afraid. Those who had seen it told the people

how the demon-possessed man had been cured. Then all the people of
the region of the Gerasenes asked Jesus to leave them, because they
were overcome with fear. So he got into the boat and left.

The man from whom the demons had gone out begged to go
with him, but Jesus sent him away, saying, "Return home and tell
how much God has done for you." So the man went away and told all
over town how much Jesus had done for him.

Before reading on, imagine you're a disciple pulling up in the boat with Jesus. What do you see? Hear? Smell? Touch?

You will see a naked man (you're so glad you didn't bring the family along on this excursion) with chains dangling, ranting in a graveyard in the cliffs by the sea. All around you are limestone caverns and rock chambers for the dead.[11]

You might hear the chains clanking or dragging in the dirt. You hear Legion offer his name. He screams at Jesus, calling him by name and begging not to be tortured. Because Legion routinely cried out in the hills, he may have been doing so when you arrived. (Perhaps you wonder how families ever had decent burial services here.)

You would smell a graveyard in ancient times. Perhaps the sea air helps clear the stench and Legion has not interrupted any of the burials; all the corpses might indeed be entombed or buried. If you get close to Legion, he probably smells of blood from the self-mutilation and cuts from the broken chains (which are painful to *look* at).

As a disciple, do you dare to touch Legion, to feel that coagulated blood in his wounds or his matted hair? Or are you clutching the boat when you realize that this man has broken those chains himself? Have you picked up anything to hold behind you as a weapon in case you need it?

Based on the man calling himself Legion (the largest unit in the

Roman army, having three thousand to six thousand soldiers) for the number of demons living in him, how scared would you be? How do you respond to Jesus, who often moved toward the "throwaways" of society: lepers, the blind and maimed, people with tattered reputations (Zacchaeus, Matthew, the woman taken in adultery, the woman at the well)? What is it like to be a disciple of Jesus on this day when you come face to face with a man you would ordinarily go out of your way to avoid?

Which of these feelings, physical responses, and thoughts might you have had toward the man?

revulsion at his appearance

pity

running away

trying not to look at his nakedness

comparing him to an animal

wishing he would go back into the hills

staring in a fascinated, morbid way at his wounds and filth

giving him a pejorative nickname — Graveyard Goliath or
  Tombstone Tobiah

fearing the man's unusual strength (to break chains)

resentment at taxpayers' money spent for guards and a supply of
  chains

other

Now look at Jesus interacting with Legion. Jesus is not intimidated by evil and its various manifestations. He courageously deals with a man you and I might hide from. How does it feel to be a disciple of a person as bold as Jesus? In what situations do you need Jesus' courage, clarity, and compassion?

Read the passage again, meditate on it, and see what happens. Keep in mind what our study has revealed, but stay open to what God wants to say to you.

After a minute or two, ask yourself, *What word or phrase or special moment or scene emerges from this passage and stays with me?*

Sit in the passage for five minutes or more and see what comes to you. Then ask yourself, *What do I sense this passage calling me to be just now?* Respond to God by praying quietly or journaling. If you wish, tell God what you most admire about the behavior of Jesus.

Ignatian meditation brings us powerfully before God as it engages our imagination and asks us to get inside Scripture. You've probably listened to a teacher or read a book where you knew that the speaker somehow "got it" in a way you didn't. That person grasped who God was and made the person of Jesus come alive to you. That sort of person has encountered God in Scripture and relished the sweetness of God's words. You can do the same thing.

Questions and Activities for Individual Reflection or Group Discussion

1. What, if anything, was said in this chapter that has made you think?

2. What interests you about the way Jesus interacted with the rich young ruler? If you wish, reread the text and ponder what speaks most to you from this scene.

3. The Ignatian method can be used with Old Testament stories, although it's most often used with the Gospels because these encounters with Jesus are so important for our formation. If you have favorite Old Testament characters or scenes you would like to meditate on using the Ignatian method, what are some of them?

4. Try the following Ignatian-style exercise. You'll notice it follows the structure of *lectio*, as most meditation does. Yet it is Ignatian

because it asks you to picture the passage, scenes, and objects mentioned. However, you may also find a word that shimmers or resonates as in *lectio*. If so, let that detail feed your meditation. If doing this meditation as an individual, read the Scripture aloud. To answer questions, you may simply think about them or wish to write responses. Ignore instructions for the group leader.

Group leader instructions for question 4: Read the previous instructions for individuals. In each section of the meditation exercise, there are instructions for the group leader. The leader should read these ahead of time to be ready to lead the group.

The Prodigal Son: Luke 15:11-24

QUIETING YOURSELF

Center yourself by breathing in and out several times. Bend your neck back and forth and then take time to let your muscles relax. Turn over each distraction as needed.

Optional warm-up question—When have you recently sensed God running toward you for some reason? If nothing comes to you, simply enjoy God's presence.

Instructions for group leader for Quieting Yourself: Read the previous centering instructions. Then present the warm-up question and let group members reflect quietly for a few minutes.

I. READING THE SCRIPTURE *(Lectio)*

Ask the Holy Spirit to speak to you through the words of the following Bible passage, and then read it aloud. If the story is familiar to you, set aside what you know about it and read each word with fresh eyes.

Instructions for group leader for lectio: Pray aloud for the Holy Spirit's leading. Suggest that group members close their eyes and listen as you read the Scripture aloud.

A WILD IDEA

Jesus continued: "There was a man who had two sons. The younger one said to his father, 'Father, give me my share of the estate.' So he divided his property between them.

"Not long after that, the younger son got together all he had, set off for a distant country and there squandered his wealth in wild living."

A SEVERE NEED

"After he had spent everything, there was a severe famine in that whole country, and he began to be in need. So he went and hired himself out to a citizen of that country, who sent him to his fields to feed pigs. He longed to fill his stomach with the pods that the pigs were eating, but no one gave him anything."

"When he came to his senses, he said, 'How many of my father's hired men have food to spare, and here I am starving to death! I will set out and go back to my father and say to him: Father, I have sinned

*against heaven and against you. I am no longer worthy to be called
your son; make me like one of your hired men.'"*

A WILD RESPONSE

*"So he got up and went to his father. But while he was still a long way
off, his father saw him and was filled with compassion for him; he
ran to his son, threw his arms around him and kissed him.*

*"The son said to him, 'Father, I have sinned against heaven and
against you. I am no longer worthy to be called your son.'*

*"But the father said to his servants, 'Quick! Bring the best robe
and put it on him. Put a ring on his finger and sandals on his feet.
Bring the fattened calf and kill it. Let's have a feast and celebrate. For
this son of mine was dead and is alive again; he was lost and is found.'
So they began to celebrate."*

Study Options

If you need to study this passage to understand it better, look at the
italicized words and phrases that follow.

give me my share of the estate—This was the same as saying, "Dad, let's
pretend you're dead. I'll take my half now." The boy could have been
executed for such rebellious behavior (see Deuteronomy 21:18-21).
"My share" would have been one third of the estate because the oldest
son got a double portion (see Deuteronomy 21:17).

pods that the pigs were eating—Because the storyteller was Jewish and
was speaking to a Jewish audience, we might assume the boy in the story
is Jewish. But Jews did not eat or sacrifice pigs, and usually wouldn't
touch them. This boy appears to have sunk so low as to have violated
the laws of his faith.

while he was still a long way off—The text doesn't say how the father could see the boy when he was far away. Did he have servants posted on the perimeter of his land? Did he stand on his roof for years? Did he have friends in town who sped off to alert him? Or did Jesus attribute to the father his own miraculous powers to see his disciples struggling from many miles away (see Mark 6:46-48)?

robe, ring, and *sandals*—The robe honored the boy. The ring gave him authority. The sandals were necessary goods. They *all* were worn by immediate family, not by servants. The father used these things to reassure his son of his love and return his dignity to him.

Instructions for group leader for Study Options: Wait a few minutes after reading the passage, then suggest participants silently read the study options.

Pondering Options

Use one or two of the following questions to prod your thinking.

1. What behavior of the father do you find most moving?

> *He didn't stop his son, but let the boy figure this out on his own.*
> *He kept watching for the boy.*
> *He wouldn't even let the boy confess what he had done wrong.*
> *He gave the boy such honor and authority after he proved he didn't deserve it.*
> *Other?*

2. What one word would you use to describe the father's behavior (for example, *selfless, eager, lavish*)?

3. Is there an empty, unproductive land of famine from which you need to return? If so, what is that land?

Instructions for group leader for Pondering Options: Ask partic-ipants to choose one pondering option and tell their answer in *one or two sentences*. Explain that this is not a time for discus-sion but for reporting responses to the questions. They may pass, if they wish.

Cues for Picturing the Passage

Before reading the passage again, consider these cues.

Cultural cue: the son's robe—As the boy headed home, he probably wore a tattered, coarse garment that swineherds customarily wore. The father offered him more than the conventional outer cloak, but put on him a long, flowing, elaborate garment (the same garment inhabitants of heaven will wear; see Revelation 6:11).[12]

Scenes to picture—Choose one or two of the following scenes and answer these questions about the scene: What do you think is going on inside the father? Inside the boy? What expressions might have been on their faces during these moments?

> *the boy asking for his inheritance*
> *the boy living a wild life, then being reduced to eating pods*
> *the father running down the trail to embrace the boy*
> *the father and the boy standing next to each other*
> *other*

> **Instructions for leader for Cues for Picturing the Passage:** Have members read the cues silently.

2. MEDITATING ON THE SCRIPTURE *(Meditatio)*

Reflect on how your life is touched by this passage today. Read the passage aloud again and ponder the following question for several minutes: *What character or scene or moment emerges from the passage and stays with you?* If you wish, write about the word, phrase, moment, or scene that resonates within you from the passage.

Reflect a while longer, and consider if God is offering you an invitation in this passage to enlarge your understanding or to do something in the next few days. What might that be? Sit quietly for a few minutes, pondering this question: *What do I need to know from this passage?*

> **Instructions for group leader for *meditatio:*** Have another group member read the passage aloud and then state the first question in italics above. Have the group sit together quietly for three or more minutes and then ask group members to say quietly the word or phrase or scene that resonates for them.
>
> Wait five minutes or so and then ask the second question in italics. Ask group members to respond by quietly saying, "I sense this passage calling me to. . ." and completing that statement with a short phrase. They may wish to speak with their eyes closed if this helps them remain focused.

3. PRAYING THE SCRIPTURE (*Oratio*)

Read the passage aloud again. Pray, perhaps using one of these suggestions:

> *Tell God how you feel about what you sensed (or didn't sense).*
> *Tell God what you most want to say at this time: "Show me how . . ."*
>   *or "Thank you for . . ."*

Instructions for group leader for *oratio:* Have another member of the group read the passage aloud. Invite members to silent prayer, perhaps using a previous suggestion.

After a few minutes, ask group members to pray for the person on their left, specifically about what the person has sensed from God. Have group members move around the circle to the right (so they'll hear clearly what is prayed for them without thinking about what they need to pray). Anyone wishing to pray silently may do so, saying, "I'm praying silently." When they're finished, they can say, "Amen."

---

4. CONTEMPLATING THE SCRIPTURE (*Contemplatio*)

Optional—Read the passage aloud again.

Take a few minutes to sit in silence and enjoy God's presence. You may wish to focus on a favorite image, such as God singing over you (see Zephaniah 3:17). If you wish, ask God, "What do you most want to say to me at this time?"

Instructions for group leader for *contemplatio:* If you wish, have the passage read aloud again. Read the previous instructions and rest in a time of contemplation. Close in prayer, thanking God for speaking to members of the group.

Chapter Eight

OTHER MEDITATIVE
APPROACHES

ENJOYING DIVERSE PATHS
INTO SCRIPTURE AND GOD'S PRESENCE

One of the questions I'm frequently asked after a meditation workshop is, how do I know if I did it right?

Consider that meditation is a skill and it gets easier the more you practice it. But even more to the point, the way people meditate varies widely. There is not one right way to meditate, but there are ways that are most helpful to you. You approach it experimentally. The important thing is to try it. When I asked one of the wisest people I know where meditation goes wrong, he said, "By never starting."

Besides, meditation is also an art. You diligently apply practiced skills but as you cooperate with God, the end results often surprise you. Do not think Scripture meditation is something over which you exercise complete control. Always stay open to the unique and personal ways the Holy Spirit wants to communicate with you.

In this chapter I offer other meditative approaches to Scripture, prayer, and all of life. Nearly all encompass the components of *lectio divina*: quieting oneself, entering into God's Word, praying, and resting in scriptural truth. Try different approaches and see what works best for your temperament and strengths. That doesn't always mean you do what is easiest for you, but in the beginning you might. Then you can refine what you do and try other methods.

PERSONALIZING THE TEXT

After reading a passage, ask yourself, *If this passage had been written to me today, what might God be telling me? If I saw the words of the Bible as a personal letter from God addressed to me, what might it say to me today?*

You may protest that this is bad scholarship—the text was addressed to someone living in a different time and different social structure. While we consider the original reader, we also know that biblical principles are universal and relevant to us today. Jesus and New Testament writers often personalized passages from the Old Testament that did indeed fit situations in the first century. To avoid errors, we apply an idea from chapter 3: Good Bible study undergirds great Scripture meditation. When you know the original, historical meaning of the text, it's easier to personalize it. You understand the principle behind it and can transfer an appropriate, immediate meaning for your life.

Approach the text as you would with *lectio divina*. Find a comfortable but alert position, quiet yourself, and ask God to send the Holy Spirit through the Word to enlighten you. Then read the passage aloud. Read it a second time, but insert your name and circumstances.

For example, read John 15 and insert your name in the blank spaces: "Abide in me, _____, as I abide in you. Just as the branch cannot bear fruit by itself unless it abides in the vine, neither can you, _____, unless you abide in me. I am the vine, you, _____, are the branches. When you abide in me and I in you, _ _ _ _ _ _, you bear much fruit, because apart from me you can do nothing. If you do not abide in me, you will be thrown away like a branch and wither; such branches are gathered, thrown into the fire, and burned. If you abide in me, and my words abide in you, ask for whatever you wish, _ _ _ _ _ _ _, and it will be done for you. My Father is glorified by this, that you, _ _ _ _ _ _ _, bear much fruit and become my disciple" (John 15:4-8, NRSV, paraphrased into second person).

As you sit in this passage, you may ponder: *How am I to abide in Christ? How will this help me bear fruit? How have I tried to do things without abiding in Christ? Why is it that those who abide in Christ receive what they ask for?*

Then respond to God in prayer and rest in what you've heard.

RANTING THROUGH A PSALM

Another way to personalize Scripture is to speak a psalm to God, but to address your concerns today. When you're angry, pray a "ranting" psalm. You may have been wise enough to walk away from a frustrating situation, but you're still angry about it. Go off by yourself and choose an imprecatory psalm—those scary ones that aren't usually read in church (Psalms 69, 77, 109, 137, to name a few.)

Back in chapter 4, we looked at Psalm 59, which David wrote when Saul had sent men to watch David's house in order to kill him. David asks for deliverance, seethes against his enemies, and alternately asks God not to kill them but to consume them in wrath (see verses 1-15). He contradicts himself, but this is normal in such an agitated state. We may want both things!

Most imprecatory psalms make a shift near the end. David made one of these shifts, ending his tirade by expressing trust in God and even praising God: "But I will sing of your strength, in the morning I will sing of your love; for you are my fortress, my refuge in times of trouble. O my Strength, I sing praise to you; you, O God, are my fortress, my loving God" (verses 16-17).

Another common shift in this psalmic pattern occurs in the last six verses of Psalm 139. We generally think of this psalm as a warm, fuzzy prayer ("you knit me together in my mother's womb," verse 13), but verses 19-22 include requests that God slay the psalmist's enemies and declarations of hate for all those who hate God. Then comes the shift: "Search me, O God, and know my heart; test me and know my anxious thoughts. See if there is any offensive way in me, and lead me in the way everlasting" (verses 23-24). This shift is not toward praise, as in Psalm 59, but toward trusting self-examination.

The shift from railing against others to examining one's own heart is like saying, "I clean up my side of the street and I let my enemy clean up his." Surrendering an enemy to God this way leads to prayer that is cleansing and then to contemplation to see if more cleansing is needed or perhaps just a word of assurance from God.

Some psalms never make any shift, which may feel too untidy for you. But consider that God is a safe place to unload such "messy" emotions. "It is better to pray badly than not to pray at all," says Eugene Peterson. "When prayed, [these psalms] are steps, first steps into the presence of God."[1] As a result, we're more likely to trust in God's deliverance.

FESTOONING

Monk, preacher, and spiritual leader Francis of Assisi (1181–1226) prayed the Lord's Prayer one phrase at a time, amplifying and expanding each phrase.[2] C. S. Lewis, a twentieth-century professor at Oxford and Cambridge Universities who explained the process of spiritual formation in his book *Mere Christianity*, did the same thing. He called it festooning, by which he meant decorating or embellishing phrases of Scripture. According to Lewis, these amplifications do not "obliterate the plain, public sense of the petition but are merely hung on it."[3]

Festooning works best on passages you've already studied or memorized. Following are examples of festoons for the Lord's Prayer. Add your ideas as you read these, but don't make it an intellectual exercise only.

After quieting yourself, pray the first phrase from the Lord's Prayer. Then add the festoons on the right. Pause. Add your own expansions of the phrase. Then festoon the next phrases the same way.

Phrase	Examples of Festooned Phrases
Our Father	Most holy, Creator, Redeemer, Savior, Comforter[4] O tender parent whose eyes never leave us
Hallowed be Thy name	Your name to us is treasured. Your name is our favorite word in our language.
Thy Kingdom come	May this earth become a place where everything you want done gets done. Thy Kingdom come . . . in my heart, in my workplace, in my nation, in this world.[5]
Thy will be done on earth as in heaven	[May we] love you with all our hearts, desiring you with all our souls, directing all our intentions to you and seeking

Phrase	Examples of Festooned Phrases
	your honor in all things. May we also love our neighbors as ourselves, drawing them to love you with all our power."[6]
Give us this day	Thank you for giving us everything we need for today. Teach us to live on the "need" level, not the "greed" level.
Lead us not into temptation	"Spare us, where possible, from crisis."[7] Help us abide in your love so temptation has no power over us.
Deliver us from evil	Help us remember that the line between good and evil runs down the middle of the human heart.

Festooning works well with familiar passages such as Psalm 23, and also with Paul's prayers, which are full of so much passion (see Ephesians 1:15-19; 3:16-21; Philippians 1:9-11; Colossians 1:9-12; 1 Thessalonians 3:12-13; 2 Thessalonians 1:11-12).

USING THE FOUR GOLDEN STRANDS

Another method of praying Scripture, which by default causes us to meditate on it, is to take a scriptural phrase that resonates with you and use it in the four kinds of prayer described in the old Baltimore Catechism: adoration, contrition, thanksgiving, and supplication (ACTS).[8] Martin Luther did this frequently, as described in Martin

Luther's Quiet Time by Walter Trobisch. This meditative way of praying Scripture "is not just petitioning, reciting and speaking. It is learning, meditating, searching and thus acquiring this perspective of eternity."[9] You may do this in any time of prayer or even during the prayer portion of lectio meditation. For example, if you were to meditatively pray Hebrews 11:16, which describes the faithful Old Testament folks who were "longing for a better country"—a heavenly one—it might sound like this:

Adoration	*Praising* God as creator of this better, unimaginable country
Contrition	*Confessing* that you often focus on the seen instead of the unseen, on getting stuff for yourself, not on loving God and advancing God's kingdom
Thanksgiving	*Thanking* God for creating this better country for you
Supplication	*Asking* God to help you to long for that better country, to long for the day when you will "know fully, even as I am fully known" (1 Corinthians 13:12)

MEDITATION IN ALL OF LIFE

Many routine activities of life can be done meditatively with an intentional focus on God speaking to you from Scripture. Here are a few ideas to get you started.

Walking Meditation

If you normally hike or take walks, use this time to meditate on Scripture. At first I took with me passages I'd printed in large type, but I finally began memorizing passages so I could hike and meditate on them without having to stop and read them (even though I'd always insisted I *couldn't* memorize).

Imagine yourself walking in the hills and saying to God,

> *Who has measured the waters in the hollow of his hand?*
> *Or with the breadth of his hand marked off the heavens?*
> *Who has held the dust of the earth in a basket,*
> *or weighed the mountains on the scales*
> *and the hills in a balance? (Isaiah 40:12)*

Can you picture God's hands holding every ocean on earth? Or God's hands spread, marking off the universe? Can you imagine God holding a basket that contains all the dust on the earth? Can you see the great mountains of the earth being weighed on one side of a scale against the other filled with all the hills?

If you're easily distracted, start by singing or humming hymns as you walk. "This Is My Father's World" or "Holy, Holy, Holy" ("all thy works declare thy name") work well outdoors. In a period of confusion or resolution, you might enjoy walking in an isolated place and belting out "Be Thou My Vision." Look for songs that express a biblical truth you need to know in the depths of your heart. Print out or memorize these as well, because confusing the verses can be distracting.

Other physical activities that lend themselves to simultaneous meditation include molding clay, crocheting, or working with wood. American Sign Language can even be a form of meditation. People enjoy watching someone sign worship music and Scripture because it helps them enter into the words.

WAKING RITUALS

When you first wake up in the morning, does your mind begin to race with what you need to do? Or maybe you ooze into the day slowly. Either way you can choose an image from Scripture to use as a waking image to sit in. For example, you might use the image from Zephaniah 3:17. See yourself sitting on the lap of God. Some mornings, perhaps after a wild dream, you may picture God rocking you to soothe you. On an event-filled day, you may see yourself as a gangly teenager on the lap of God, struggling to run around and get going, but God holding you gently, quieting "you with his love."

If you're ready for a more elaborate waking ritual, consider letting your first thoughts be to meditate on the Lord's Prayer or Psalm 23— something you know by heart. If it's a particularly anxious time in your life, you can take each phrase of Psalm 23 and add "no matter what." The Lord is my shepherd . . . no matter what. I have everything I need . . . no matter what. He leads me beside still waters . . . no matter what. He restores my soul . . . no matter what. I will fear no evil . . . no matter what. For you are with me . . . no matter what.

INTERACTING WITH CREATION

According to the book of Psalms, the objects of our meditation include God's unfailing love, precepts, decrees, statutes, and promises (see Psalms 48:9; 119:15,23,48,78,97,99,148). These refer primarily to Scripture, which is what this book is about. But the Psalms mention meditating also on God's works and wonders. These are found not only in Scripture, but also in creation.

> • *"I will* meditate *on all your works and* consider *all your mighty deeds"* (Psalm 77:12, *emphasis added*).
> • *"Let me understand the teaching of your precepts; then I will meditate on your wonders"* (119:27, *emphasis added*).
> • *"I* remember *the days of long ago; I* meditate *on all your works and* consider *what your hands have done"* (143:5, *emphasis added*).
> • *"They will speak of the glorious splendor of your majesty, and I will meditate on your wonderful works"* (145:5, *emphasis added*).

How do we meditate on God's works and wonders? The Psalms show us: "When I consider your heavens, the work of your fingers, the moon and the stars, which you have set in place, what is man that you are mindful of him, the son of man that you care for him?" (Psalm 8:3-4). So we *consider* the works and wonder of creation around us. Jesus apparently reflected on creation a great deal, using these insights in his teaching.

You can do this while gardening, walking, practicing the forgotten art of porch-sitting, or even by trying what has been called "crabgrass contemplation." First choose an outdoor area. It doesn't have to be a beautiful, plant-filled place, but if it is, the experience may be more interesting. Walk, keeping a slow pace and taking deep breaths. Ask God to speak to you. Look intently at everything around you. Notice what draws your attention. Stay open to everything around you. Don't mull over your own thoughts. Hear every sound. Stop and feel things— edges of leaves and the texture of bark. Rub your hand against the ground. Compare the many shades of green with each other and notice how different they are. Smell things to see if they have a scent. Explore each thing you see and thank God for it.[10]

BLENDING THE DISCIPLINES

Perhaps you've noticed that meditation overlaps with other disciplines, especially prayer. *Lectio* involves a time of formal prayer, but meditation may at any moment become prayer. Prayer invades meditation, so to speak.

The opposite is also true. Meditation invades prayer as well as our entire thought life. Without trying to do so, those who meditate often use words of Scripture in prayer or conversation because

> *Scripture becomes so deeply embedded in our lives that it need not be "drawn out" and "thought about" to have an influence. It becomes part of our very soul. It shapes us and conforms to us. Its very contours become the contours of our thoughts, words and hopes. This is beyond the stage where Scripture is used to extract comforting verses or even "principles of living." To internalize the Scripture means that it becomes so much a part of us that the text begins to "play" with us and . . . Scripture becomes our most engaging conversation partner.*[11]

For example, when Jesus supposedly quoted Psalm 22:1 on the cross (see Matthew 27:46), we have to question the use of the word "quote." Did Jesus simply quote it or was this psalm so embedded in his soul, so much a part of how Jesus thought and spoke that in a moment of anguish these words burst forth from his heart? Such spur-of-the-moment Scripture-drenched responses occur when we have meditated on Scripture. It becomes our personal language and customary pattern of the way we talk to God and about God.

These solitary disciplines of meditation and prayer even cross over to the more active ones. If we serve and pray at the same time (practicing the presence of God), we avoid becoming so task oriented that we run over people. We avoid patting ourselves on the back because we're doing such a great job. Dietrich Bonhoeffer knew this truth, so he required seminarians to spend a half-hour each morning for a week meditating on the same passage. The rest of the day was devoted to work. "And in the *it* of work," Bonhoeffer explained, you may find the "Thou of God. All of life becomes your prayer."[12]

Disciplines also affect each other, and one of the benefits of meditation is how it affects the way you study. You will become more attentive and alert and not as likely to try to "master" the text. In fact you may find that you study meditatively. Dallas Willard describes meditative study this way: "You come to the Word and say, *Let it speak to me, even if it contradicts anything I believe.* You read a text with openness, repentance, and humility, thinking, *Let it speak to me, even if it contradicts anything I believe.*"[13] Instead of reading to find proof texts (statements that back up what we already think is true), we read with an open mind and heart and ask ourselves, *What does this say that I need to know about God? About myself? What do I think I know that needs correction? Is there something I've missed?*[14] These questions are also excellent to keep in mind when listening to a sermon or reading a book. That way we listen meditatively for God to speak instead of evaluating and criticizing the speaker or writer.

If we read or hear something different from what we're used to, we bring it before God, compare it with commentaries, and discuss it with other disciples of Jesus. Then we wait on God until the dots connect.

After you learn to meditate, study will also be different because you will be used to putting yourself in the shoes of people in Scripture and they will be real to you. When you read a passage, it will be like hearing words from someone you know, and you'll connect it to other things you know about that person. For example, you'll read the book of James and wonder if any of those ideas come from his life as a kid watching his big brother run the carpentry business. You'll be aghast that Nehemiah had the energy and resources to put up with the sabotage in rebuilding the Jerusalem walls, but then you'll remember that he had been schooled in the politics of the Persian palace. You'll stagger at how Paul became so dramatically opposite of the know-it-all Pharisee he used to be. Because you're used to concentrating more diligently, your mind will connect the dots between what you're studying and what you already know.

I have often been amazed by how a passage of Scripture speaks to some situation I'm not even consciously thinking about. Once while meditating on Jesus washing the disciples' feet, I found I was angry that none of the disciples would take on the foot-washing work of the servants. (Apparently no servants were present to do this, so who would do it?) Jesus surprised them and did it himself. I loved Jesus' can-do, no-nonsense approach. He picked up the towel and did the lowly task without making a big deal out of it. What a class act!

In contemplation I saw myself at the airport, a place I hated to be. I fly a lot for speaking engagements, but I disliked flying intensely because it's so confining. I felt cramped and suffocated in the breathing space of strangers who liked to watch what I wrote on my laptop computer. Flying was indeed part of my service of leading retreats, but I resented even being in an airport. I used to watch people (especially older folks) drop something and no one would help them. We all waited to see if that person really needed help.

In the quiet of this meditation I got a new vision for airport behavior. Maybe I was supposed to be there to help people—especially older people. So that became my job. The next day I had to fly and I looked for opportunities to help people. When someone dropped something, I sidled up behind, picked up the object, handed it to him, and scooted away without a word. When another person struggled to get her luggage in the overhead bin, I jumped up, shoved it in, and sat down. I admired so much Jesus' silent but compassionate and practical ways in the foot-washing passage, and they "leaked" into my life. I no longer hate being at an airport.

This book isn't about meditation as much as it's about trusting God and letting God transform you. You may find that as you meditate, your interactive life with God will increase. As you interact more regularly and personally, you will come to trust God more. As you have more confidence in God, you will change without trying so hard. Branches that abide in the vine automatically bear fruit. As you do the connecting, God will do the perfecting. You will become more like Christ—free of contempt and anger, free of domination by greed or sexual lust, free of the desire to dominate and control verbally, free of grudges and payback, free to love enemies, free to serve without being a star, free from the longing to have more money or be better looking than someone else. This kind of transformation happens as God "modifies our perception, changes our vision of the world. God actually gets into our soul and moves things around. Things don't mean the same thing as they used to," Willard says.[15]

So even though you've finished reading the text of this book, you are invited to keep meditating on Scripture. Appendix B, "Meditation Exercises," contains exercises to help you experiment more and learn how to meditate without the help of any book. You may use each meditation exercise many times, because as you change and grow, the Scripture passage will speak to you differently each time. The next time you meditate on the passage you focused on today, you will be undergoing different difficulties, will be involved in different situations, or will have come to a new place of understanding. As a result, you will hear something different and Scripture will be ever fresh and new.

Questions and Activities for Individual Reflection or Group Discussion

1. What, if anything, was said in this chapter that has made you think?

2. To practice personalizing, paraphrase John 17 so that Jesus is praying

this prayer for you at this moment. Change or omit whatever words or verses do not apply to you. (If you wish, tape record yourself reading this differently worded prayer and then listen to it. Close your eyes and imagine Jesus praying for you today.[16]) After reading the passage this way, move to prayer and then to contemplation.

3. In what trying situation might it help you to get away and rant a psalm?

4. Try festooning Psalm 23. Take each phrase and pray the phrase. Then expand on it.

5. To try the four golden strands method, choose a verse of Scripture that fascinates you. Pray it through the four strands of adoration, confession, thanksgiving, and supplication.

Group leader instructions: Omit question 2 and have someone in your group read John 15 aloud to the group (in the previous text), pausing at the blank spaces so participants can whisper their names as the passage is read. Allow a time of quiet and then ask, "What do you sense God saying to you in this passage?"

For question 4, have one person read a phrase from Psalm 23 and then as many as wish can add festoons. Do this as a prayer, with eyes closed.

For question 5, choose a verse and quiet yourselves for prayer. Then have someone read the verse and ask for prayers of adoration. When the group is finished with adoration phrases, continue the same way with confession, thanksgiving, and supplication.

GUIDELINES FOR GROUP MEDITATION

🌿

The ideal size for a group is from two to six people. That way participants can sit in a close circle so they can hear each other well and so they won't have to speak loudly. If you have more than that, split into two groups.

QUESTIONS TO CONSIDER

If a designated leader facilitates the group, the following issues need to be decided before the first session. If there is no designated leader and leadership rotates among group members, the group itself needs to decide the following issues.

- *How many sessions will there be? (There are meditation exercises in appendix B, as well as partial exercises at the ends of chapters 4 and 5, and full exercises at the end of chapters 6 and 7.)*
- *How frequent will the sessions be? Weekly? Biweekly? Monthly?*
- *Which sections of meditations will be used? Besides the four sections*

of lectio, will the group use optional warm-up questions, study options, pondering options, and cues for picturing the passage?

• How much time will be needed for each session? The meditation exercises are designed for a forty- to sixty-minute session, depending on how many participants you have and how long they take to respond. Leaders need to process sections themselves (such as study options, meditation, or contemplation) and then observe participants to see how long they need to process them. (Group members may simply look up when they are finished.) In sections that ask for a response (optional warm-up questions, pondering options, praying the passage), participants often need to take time answering and some may choose not to respond. Ask God to guide you in knowing when to continue.

• Where will the group meet? If possible, meet in the same place every week. If childcare will be provided, it's helpful if it takes place at another site.

• May newcomers join the group? If so, explain the importance of silence and talking slowly. Go over the following group participation guidelines with newcomers.

• Which of the group participation guidelines will be used?

If leadership is rotating among all group members, change leaders weekly. Remember that leaders in this sort of study are not experts. What makes a good leader is willingness to be yourself and being open to God's Spirit. Besides using the instructions to group leaders, leaders can use as much of the instructions to individuals as they wish. They may have to remind participants occasionally to stay within the structure: "Only two sentences, please." Also, if a leader isn't used to silent meditation, it's important to time each segment carefully. In the beginning especially, thirty seconds of silence may seem like five minutes.

GROUP PARTICIPATION GUIDELINES

In the beginning, these should be read at the start of each group meeting.

Openness—I will be as candid and honest as I am able. I understand this group is a safe place in which I can admit strong emotions, confess faults, and reveal insights that may seem outlandish.

Confidentiality—I will not tell anyone outside the group what someone else said in the group—not even spouses or absent group members. I may tell someone what I said, but not what someone else said.

Acceptance—I will avoid judging, giving advice, or criticizing, even if it's only in my mind—*He is way off! She's never going to plug into meditation!* I will try to turn this self-talk into a prayer for the person and then focus on the passage in front of me.

Talking within the group—I understand that this is not a traditional discussion-oriented Bible study. I come together with others not to have extended conversation but for the community experience of seeking God. I will abide by instructions to comment only briefly. If something about the passage bothers me, I can discuss it with someone else later.

Wonder—I expect other group members to sense insights that are different from mine. God meets each of us in the places that still need to conform with the image of Christ. For each of us, those places are different. I will make allowances for differences in temperament, timing, and needs. Passages about metaphors and images resonate better with some people; others relate better to Bible characters; still others like the silence best. I will enjoy the wonder of how God speaks to each of us as special children.

Privacy—If I am unable to answer a question aloud because no answer comes to me or I'm unwilling to reveal my answer to the group, I may say "pass" and offer no explanation.

Attentiveness—I will try to attend the group meetings and be open to the needs of others when I am there.

Hints and Reminders

You may wish to read the following before each group session begins if participants are new to meditation.

- *It helps participants to stay focused if they keep their eyes closed or stare at a blank wall.*
- *It helps participants if all use as few words as possible and speak quietly and unhurriedly. Don't chatter or do anything that draws attention to yourself.*
- *As participants listen to each other, it helps to think, I am listening with the heart of God. Other members of the group have the responsibility to receive what each person says respectfully and prayerfully. Don't evaluate, asking yourself, How come she said that? Don't think about how your answer sounds compared to another's. Picture that person being cherished by God.*
- *Avoid "crosstalk." Do not question each other or comment on others' ideas. If you believe someone is wrong or misunderstanding a passage, let the Holy Spirit have a chance to speak to that person. Pray for the person, but do not interrupt.*
- *The words or phrases shared by participants should come from the passage. Don't choose a word or phrase; let it come to you. That word or phrase may change during the session.*
- *No one is required to say anything. A participant can say "pass" if he or she doesn't wish to speak. Anything said is a gift to the group.*
- *Expect many pauses and much silence in these sessions. Do not become nervous about it. Understand that silence is good.*

- *Those who read the passage aloud should strive not to emphasize any word in particular. It's amazing how God uses "insignificant" words to speak to people. Therefore readers should go over the passage so they read it clearly without stumbling, but they should avoid reading it conversationally or dramatically.*

AN ALTERNATE FORMAT

Group *lectio* has also been done in the same format, but nothing is spoken aloud. Participants sit in a small circle as before. The leader walks them through the steps with different readers, but answers to all questions and all prayers are silent. Then at the end, the leader invites the members to share with other group members what word or phrase resonated with them and what they heard God say to them.

An excellent book that explains how to do group *lectio* is *Gathered in the Word* by Norvene Vest (Upper Room, 1996). She has researched Benedictine spirituality, and the method she recommends is faithful to tradition yet responsive to contemporary needs.

MEDITATION EXERCISES

FINDING INTIMACY WITH GOD

See also:

> *Ephesians 3:16-21, a prayer about grasping the love of God (chapter 2)*
> *Luke 15:11-24, the parable of the prodigal son (chapter 7)*

Elijah Runs Away to God: 1 Kings 19:3-13,15-16

QUIETING YOURSELF

Center yourself by breathing in and out several times. Bend your neck back and forth and let your muscles relax. Turn over each distraction as needed. Be still, and know that God is God.

Optional warm-up question—If you're having trouble settling down, consider this question: What kinds of experiences make you feel like saying, "I have had enough, Lord"?

If nothing comes to you, simply enjoy God's presence.

Instructions for group leader for Quieting Yourself: Read the previous centering instructions. After presenting the warm-up question, let participants reflect quietly for a few minutes. Repeat the question and ask them to share their thoughts in a sentence or two. Anyone who wishes to pass may do so.

1. READING THE SCRIPTURE (*Lectio*)

Ask the Holy Spirit to speak to you through the words of the following Bible passage, and then read it aloud. If the story is familiar to you, set aside what you know about it and read each word with fresh eyes.

Instructions for group leader for *lectio:* Pray as directed previously. Follow the previous instructions, suggesting that group members close their eyes and listen as you read the Scripture aloud.

DESPAIR

Elijah was afraid and ran for his life. . . . He . . . went a day's journey into the desert. He came to a broom tree, sat down under it and prayed that he might die. "I have had enough, LORD," he said. "Take my life; I am no better than my ancestors."

TENDER MERCIES

Then he lay down under the tree and fell asleep.

All at once an angel touched him and said, "Get up and eat." He looked around, and there by his head was a cake of bread baked over hot coals, and a jar of water. He ate and drank and then lay down again.

The angel of the LORD came back a second time and touched him and said, "Get up and eat, for the journey is too much for you." So he got up and ate and drank. Strengthened by that food, he traveled forty days and forty nights until he reached Horeb, the mountain of God. There he went into a cave and spent the night.

CONVERSATION WITH THE ALMIGHTY

And the word of the LORD came to him: "What are you doing here, Elijah?"

He replied, "I have been very zealous for the LORD God Almighty. The Israelites have rejected your covenant, broken down your altars, and put your prophets to death with the sword. I am the only one left, and now they are trying to kill me too."

The LORD said, "Go out and stand on the mountain in the presence of the LORD, for the LORD is about to pass by."

Then a great and powerful wind tore the mountains apart and shattered the rocks before the LORD, but the LORD was not in the wind. After the wind there was an earthquake, but the LORD was not in the earthquake. After the earthquake came a fire, but the LORD was not in the fire. And after the fire came a gentle whisper. When Elijah heard it, he pulled his cloak over his face and went out and stood at the mouth of the cave. . . .

The LORD *said to him, "Go back the way you came, and . . .*
anoint Hazael king over Aram . . . anoint Jehu son of Nimshi king
over Israel, and anoint Elisha son of Shaphat from Abel Meholah to
succeed you as prophet."

Study Options

If you need to study this passage to understand it better, look at the following italicized words and phrases.

was afraid—Ahab and Jezebel, monarchs of Israel, worshiped Baal, a foreign god that Elijah prophesied against. Elijah challenged the prophets of Baal to a contest in which Elijah proved God's power by calling down fire from heaven on his sacrifice. Baal's prophets got no response for their sacrifice and "lost" the contest. After this stunning victory, however, Jezebel angrily threatened Elijah's life.

traveled forty days and forty nights—Elijah ran the length of Israel from north to south (ninety miles). From there, he ran to Mount Horeb in the southern tip of Arabia (two hundred to three hundred miles, depending on the route).[1]

Horeb—Another name for Mount Sinai, where God conversed with Moses centuries earlier.

only one left—Jezebel had ordered the death of all the Lord's prophets (see 1 Kings 18:4).

anoint—To set aside for a special purpose, one of the many prophetic duties which were Elijah's to do.

Elisha—This man went on to become Elijah's famous protégé who performed many miracles and managed to see God's chariots of fire coming to help when no one else could (see 2 Kings 6:17).

> **Instructions for group leader for Study Options:** Wait a few min-
> utes after reading the passage, then suggest participants silently
> read Study Options.

Pondering Options

Use one or two of the following questions to prod your thinking about God's interaction with Elijah.

1. It's difficult to understand how Elijah could be so intimidated by Jezebel after he'd just won the tremendous victory over the prophets of Baal. Can you think of other reasons Elijah might have been so afraid?

    - *Emotional highs (such as defeating the prophets of Baal) can beget emotional lows.*
    - *He felt alone without the other prophets of God.*
    - *He'd endured a lot, and this was the last straw.*
    - *He had thought Ahab and Jezebel would give in, but they didn't.*
    - *Other*

2. Put yourself in Elijah's place. Which of these experiences would have been most emotionally draining for you?

    - *receiving a death threat*
    - *making a long journey on foot*
    - *feeling suicidal*
    - *encountering an angel*

3. Which of the details about the angel's service to Elijah is most mean-
    ingful to you? What do they tell us about how God relates to us?

    > • *The angel respected Elijah's need for rest and made it possible.*
    > • *The angel prepared hot baked bread for him.*
    > • *The meal the angel provided was substantial enough to sustain
    >   Elijah for forty days—a miraculous power bar, of sorts.*
    > • *The angel provided conversation.*

4. While Elijah was in the cave, God asked him, "What are you doing
    here, Elijah?" God obviously knew the answer, so why do you think
    God asked him the question?

5. Elijah was experienced enough in the ways of God to recognize
    God's voice in the gentle whisper instead of thinking that God was
    speaking in the rock-shattering wind, earthquake, or fire. What
    makes a person good at hearing God that way?

6. Part of how God responded to the discouraged prophet was to give
    him jobs to do, including the anointing of a successor, Elisha. Elijah
    and Elisha bonded to the point that it seems likely that Elijah never
    again felt he was "the only one left." Has there been a time when
    you felt lonely, but God provided you with unexpected sources of
    joy and companionship? If so, when?

Instructions for group leader for Pondering Options: After the
passage is read, ask group members to read silently the previous
material. They may journal, if they wish. After a few minutes, have
them choose one pondering option and tell their answer in *one
sentence or two.*

Cues for Picturing the Passage

Before reading the passage again, consider these cues.

Setting cue: Elijah under the tree—Picture Elijah, bewildered and sitting under a broom tree—a large shrub that can grow up to thirteen feet high.[2] Picture him with his garment made of hair and a girdle (wide belt). He has just made a two-hundred-mile journey to Mount Horeb across wild, barren wilderness. (See 2 Kings 1:8.)

Scenes to picture:

- *Elijah running or Elijah sitting under the tree*
- *God providing Elijah tender mercies: sleep, food, and sympathy*
- *Elijah watching the great and powerful wind tearing the mountains apart and shattering the rocks; the earthquake and the fire; then finally the gentle whisper*

Instructions for leader for Cues for Picturing the Passage:

Have members read the cues silently.

---

2. MEDITATING ON THE SCRIPTURE *(Meditatio)*

Reflect on how your life is touched by this passage today. Read the passage aloud again and ponder the following question for several minutes: *What word or phrase or scene or moment emerges from the passage and stays with you?*

Reflect a while longer, and consider if God is offering you an invitation in this passage to enlarge your understanding or to do something in the next few days. Ponder this question: *What do I need to know from this passage?*

Instructions for group leader for *meditatio:* Have another group member read the passage aloud and then state the first question printed in italics previously. Have the group sit together quietly for three minutes or more and then ask group members to say the word or phrase or scene that resonates for them.

Wait for five or more minutes and then ask the second question in italics. Ask group members to respond by saying, "I sense this passage calling me to . . . " and then completing that statement with a short phrase.

---

3. PRAYING THE SCRIPTURE (*Oratio*)

Read the passage aloud again. Pray, perhaps using one of these suggestions:

- *Tell God how you feel about what you sensed (or didn't sense).*
- *Tell God what you most want to say at this time: "Show me how . . ."
  or "Thank you for . . ."*

If you wish, take the idea of the passage that spoke to you and within that idea find one or two of the following:

- *something for which to praise God*
- *something for which you need to thank God*
- *a fault you need to confess*
- *a request for yourself*
- *a request for others*

Instructions for group leader for *oratio:* Have another member of the group read the passage aloud. Invite members to pray silently, perhaps using the previous prayer suggestions.

After a few minutes, ask group members to pray for the person on their left. Anyone wishing to pray silently may do so, saying, "I'm praying silently." When they're finished, they can say, "Amen."

---

4. CONTEMPLATING THE SCRIPTURE (*Contemplatio*)

Optional—Read the passage aloud again.

Take a few minutes to sit in silence and enjoy God's presence. You may wish to use a favorite image. If you wish, ask, "God, what is it you most want to say to me at this time?"

Instructions for group leader for *contemplatio:* If you wish, have the passage read aloud again. Read the previous instructions and enjoy a time of contemplation. Close in prayer, thanking God for speaking to members of the group.

HEALING LIFE'S WOUNDS

See also:

- Luke 13:10-17, Jesus healing the bent-over woman (chapter 7)
- Mark 5:22-34, Jesus healing the woman with the issue of blood
  (chapter 4)

The Satisfied Heart: Luke 12:22-34

QUIETING YOURSELF

Center yourself by breathing in and out several times. Use the "palms down, palms up" method described in chapter 4; but this time, name the things that worry you, and turn your palms upward to surrender them. Then sit for a few minutes with your palms turned upward.

Instructions for group leader for Quieting Yourself: Read the previous centering instructions and let group members reflect quietly for a few minutes.

---

1. READING THE SCRIPTURE (*Lectio*)

Ask the Holy Spirit to speak to you through the words of the following Bible passage, and then read it aloud.

Instructions for group leader for *lectio:* Follow the previous instructions, suggesting that group members close their eyes and listen as you read the Scripture aloud.

WASTED WORRY

Then Jesus said to his disciples: "Therefore I tell you, do not worry about your life, what you will eat; or about your body, what you will wear. Life is more than food, and the body more than clothes. Consider the ravens: They do not sow or reap, they have no store-room or barn; yet God feeds them. And how much more valuable you are than birds! Who of you by worrying can add a single hour to his life? Since you cannot do this very little thing, why do you worry about the rest?

"Consider how the lilies grow. They do not labor or spin. Yet I tell you, not even Solomon in all his splendor was dressed like one of these. If that is how God clothes the grass of the field, which is here today, and tomorrow is thrown into the fire, how much more will he clothe you, O you of little faith!"

THE FOCUSED HEART

"And do not set your heart on what you will eat or drink; do not worry about it. For the pagan world runs after all such things, and your Father knows that you need them. But seek his kingdom, and these things will be given to you as well.

"Do not be afraid, little flock, for your Father has been pleased to give you the kingdom. Sell your possessions and give to the poor. Provide purses for yourselves that will not wear out, a treasure in heaven that will not be exhausted, where no thief comes near and no moth destroys. For where your treasure is, there your heart will be also."

Pondering Options

Use one or two of the following methods to prod your thinking.

Become one of Jesus' listeners—Put yourself in the place of Jesus' listeners. How would you have felt about his two humorous images?

> • *somebody tallying up the additional hours they can live because they invested their time worrying*
> • *people adoring lilies more than the most popular movie star*

Jesus also used three paradoxes to illustrate God's great power:

> • *ravens who store up nothing, yet have what they need*
> • *unstealable treasure*
> • *purses that don't wear out*

Paradoxes make us ask, "How can this be? How can a raven store nothing yet have necessities? How can treasure be burglarproof? How can a purse, worn often for buying and trading, not get old and develop holes?" These paradoxes cannot be explained because they're mysteries of God's provisions.

Refresh these paradoxical solutions so you can get a keener idea of how mesmerized Jesus' listeners were by his paradoxes. Consider something you worry about (staying physically fit, having sufficient retirement funds, resolving problems with other people, raising kids who succeed) and make up a mysterious solution to it like the ones in the following chart.

Worry	Paradoxical Solution
How will I stay physically fit?	an adult body that builds muscles even when you're asleep
Will I have sufficient retirement funds?	a pension that doubles every time you take a sick day

Personalize the passage—Jesus said, "Life is more than food, and the body more than clothes" (verse 23). If Jesus had spoken that verse to you, he would have known what you treasure and used it in the place of "food." If so, how would Jesus have completed that sentence to have riveted you: Life is more than _____. Clothing? Looking attractive? Having a happy life? Achieving goals? Scratching off every item on today's "to do" list?

Picture the satisfied heart—Jesus seemed preoccupied with the heart—telling listeners where to "set their hearts" and looking at where their heart "is." The Greek word for "heart," *kardia*, came to stand for a person's "mental and moral activity, both the rational and emotional elements. . . . the heart is used figuratively for the hidden springs of the personal life."[3]

In the following verses, what words would you substitute for the word *heart?* Energy? Focus? Purpose?

> *"And do not set your* heart *on what you will eat or drink; do not worry about it"* (verse 29, emphasis added).
> *"For where your treasure is, there your* heart *will be also"* (verse 34, emphasis added).

Consider the beliefs of the heart—The satisfied heart believes

- *God will provide whatever is needed. What does the worried heart believe?*
- *Life is more than food. What does the worried heart believe?*
- *If I seek God's kingdom, all the food and drink I need will be provided. What does the worried heart believe?*
- *God provides treasures that can't be taken away. What does the worried heart believe?*

Instructions for group leader for Pondering Options: After the passage is read, ask group members to read silently the previous material, jotting down thoughts in a journal if they wish. After a few minutes, have them choose one pondering option and share their response in a sentence or two. Explain that this is not a time for discussion but for reporting brief responses to the questions. Then have group members read the cues silently.

Cues for Picturing the Passage

Before reading the passage again, consider this cue.

Cultural cue: Solomon in all his splendor—Solomon was considered a fashionable, glamorous person. To get the meaning, we might substitute the name of a rich, classy person or a model.

> **Instructions for group leader for Cues for Picturing the Passage:**
> Have members read the cue silently. When they're finished reading, continue.

2. MEDITATING ON THE SCRIPTURE (*Meditatio*)

Reflect on how your life is touched by this passage today. Read the passage aloud again and ponder the following question for several minutes: *What word or phrase emerges from the passage and stays with you?* Reflect a while longer, and consider if God is offering you an invitation in this passage to enlarge your understanding or to do something in the next few days. What might that be? Sit quietly for a few minutes, pondering this question: *What do I need to know from this passage?*

> **Instructions for group leader for *meditatio:*** Have another group member read the passage aloud and then state the first question printed in italics above. Have the group sit together quietly for three minutes or more, and then ask group members to say the word or phrase or scene that resonates for them. Remind them that they may pass if they wish.
>
> Wait for five minutes or more. Ask the second question in italics. Ask group members to respond by saying, "I sense this passage calling me to . . . " and then completing that statement with a short phrase.

3. PRAYING THE SCRIPTURE (*Oratio*)

Read the passage aloud again. Pray, perhaps using one of these suggestions:

- *Tell God how you feel about what you sensed (or didn't sense).*
- *Tell God what you most want to say at this time: "Show me how . . ."*
  or "Thank you for . . ."

Take the idea of the passage that spoke to you and within that idea find

- *something for which to praise God*
- *something for which you need to thank God*
- *a fault you need to confess*
- *a request for yourself*
- *a request for others*

Instructions for group leader for *oratio:* Have another member of the group read the passage aloud. Invite members to pray silently, perhaps using a previous suggestion.

After a few minutes, ask group members to pray for the person on their left. Anyone wishing to pray silently may do so, saying, "I'm praying silently." When they're finished, they can say, "Amen."

4. CONTEMPLATING THE SCRIPTURE (*Contemplatio*)

Optional—Read the passage aloud again.

Take a few minutes to sit in silence and enjoy God's presence. If you wish, ask, "God, what is it you most want to say to me at this time?"

Instructions for group leader for *contemplatio:* If you wish, have the passage read aloud again. Read the previous instructions and enjoy a time of contemplation. Close in prayer, thanking God for speaking to members of the group.

Jesus Heals the Caregiver Too: Mark 9:14-27

QUIETING YOURSELF

Center yourself by breathing in and out several times. Bend your neck back and forth and then take time to let your muscles relax. Turn over each distraction as needed.

Optional warm-up question—If you're having trouble settling down, consider this question: If you've had experiences as a caregiver to a child, a younger sibling, an aging relative, or an injured spouse, what have those experiences been like for you?

- *I sensed God's comfort at times.*
- *It was draining.*
- *It encroached on my life.*
- *It made me cry at times.*
- *It felt like God's work at times.*
- *Other*

> **Instructions for group leader for Quieting Yourself:** Read the previous centering instructions. After presenting the warm-up question, let participants reflect quietly for a few minutes. Repeat the question and ask them to share their thoughts in a sentence or two. Anyone who wishes to pass may do so.

1. READING THE SCRIPTURE *(Lectio)*

Ask the Holy Spirit to speak to you through the words of the following Bible passage, and then read it aloud.

> **Instructions for group leader for *lectio:*** Follow the previous instructions, suggesting that group members close their eyes and listen as you read the Scripture aloud.

THE ARGUING ONLOOKERS

When they came to the other disciples, they saw a large crowd around them and the teachers of the law arguing with them. As soon as all the people saw Jesus, they were overwhelmed with wonder and ran to greet him.

"What are you arguing with them about?" he asked.

THE FATHER-CAREGIVER

*A man in the crowd answered, "Teacher, I brought you my son, who
is possessed by a spirit that has robbed him of speech. Whenever it
seizes him, it throws him to the ground. He foams at the mouth,
gnashes his teeth and becomes rigid. I asked your disciples to drive out
the spirit, but they could not."*

*"O unbelieving generation," Jesus replied, "how long shall I stay
with you? How long shall I put up with you? Bring the boy to me."*

*So they brought him. When the spirit saw Jesus, it immediately
threw the boy into a convulsion. He fell to the ground and rolled
around, foaming at the mouth.*

Jesus asked the boy's father, "How long has he been like this?"

*"From childhood," he answered. "It has often thrown him into
fire or water to kill him. But if you can do anything, take pity on us
and help us."*

*"'If you can'?" said Jesus. "Everything is possible for him who
believes."*

*Immediately the boy's father exclaimed, "I do believe; help me
overcome my unbelief!"*

THE HEALED SON

*When Jesus saw that a crowd was running to the scene, he rebuked
the evil spirit. "You deaf and mute spirit," he said, "I command you,
come out of him and never enter him again."*

*The spirit shrieked, convulsed him violently and came out. The
boy looked so much like a corpse that many said, "He's dead." But
Jesus took him by the hand and lifted him to his feet, and he stood up.*

Study Options

If you need to study this passage to understand it better, look at the following italicized words and phrases.

teachers of the law—The scribes had tried to discredit Jesus, and now they had his disciples in an uproar, unable to show Jesus' authority and power as the Son of God.

possessed by a spirit—A spirit from the enemy controlled this boy's actions, giving him symptoms similar to epilepsy.

unbelieving generation—Jesus was often disappointed and exasperated at the lack of faith and hardness of hearts of the disciples (see Mark 4:40; 6:50-52; 8:17-21), who had already cast out demons successfully (see Mark 6:13).

Instructions for group leader for Study Options: Wait a few minutes after reading the passage, then suggest participants silently read Study Options.

Pondering Options

Use one or both of the following questions to reflect on.

1. Jesus engaged the father in conversation (asking him a question he undoubtedly already knew the answer to), showing concern for the caregiver as well as the possessed boy. When would it have helped you as a caregiver if someone had shown concern for you?

2. How does Jesus respond to the father's admission of his doubts: "If you can do anything, take pity on us and help us"; "I do believe; help me overcome my unbelief!"

Instructions for group leader for Pondering Options: After the passage is read, ask group members to read silently the previous material and jot down any thoughts in a journal, if they wish. After a few minutes, have them choose one pondering option and tell their answer in *one sentence or two*. Remind them that this is not a time for discussion, but for reporting responses to the questions. They may pass, if they wish.

Cues for Picturing the Passage

Scenes to picture: The boy—Gather all the scriptural descriptions of the boy so you can picture him:

- *dusty, with dirt matted in the foam from his mouth (verse 20)*
- *may have burn marks on his body because the demon had been thrown into fires since he was a child (verse 22)*
- *probably also bore the marks of battering from convulsions and being thrown into water, where he may have fallen on rocks (verses 20, 22)*
- *hearing the noise of the crowd and his own voice for the first time (verse 25)*

Keep in mind all the viewpoints from which you might picture this scene:

- the teachers of the law—*Their primary interest was orthodoxy. They were concerned about this upstart preacher, Jesus, who didn't do things the conventional way of the Pharisees.*

- the disciples—*Their primary interest was casting out a demon, which they had seen Jesus do many times. They were probably self-conscious and frustrated at not being able to cast out the demon. After all, Jesus commanded them to do so (see Matthew 10:8) and had given them authority to do so (see Mark 3:15).*
- the father of the demon-possessed boy—*He wanted his son healed. He had watched the boy be tortured for a long time.*
- the boy—*He had lived a noiseless life since childhood. He had been battered and burned. People talked to each other, but not to him.*

Instructions for group leader for Cues for Picturing the Passage: Have members read the cues silently. When they're finished reading, continue.

---

2. MEDITATING ON THE SCRIPTURE (*Meditatio*)

Reflect on how your life is touched by this passage today. Read the passage aloud again and ponder the following question for several minutes: *What character or scene or moment emerges from the passage and stays with you?* Reflect a while longer, and consider if God is offering you an invitation in this passage to enlarge your understanding or to do something in the next few days. What might that be? Sit quietly for a few minutes, pondering this question: *What do I need to know from this passage?*

Instructions for group leader for *meditatio:* Have another group member read the passage aloud and then state the first question printed in italics previously. Have the group sit together quietly for three minutes or more and then ask group members to say the word or phrase or scene that resonates for them. Remind them that they may pass if they wish.

Wait for five minutes or so and then ask the second question in italics. Ask group members to respond by saying, "I sense this passage calling me to . . ." and then completing that statement with a short phrase.

3. PRAYING THE SCRIPTURE (*Oratio*)

Read the passage aloud again. Pray, perhaps using one of these suggestions:

- *Tell God how you feel about what you sensed (or didn't sense).*
- *Tell God what you most want to say at this time: "Show me how . . ." or "Thank you for . . ."*

Instructions for group leader for *oratio:* Have another member of the group read the passage aloud. Invite members to pray silently, perhaps using the previous prayer suggestions.

After a few minutes, ask group members to pray for the person on their left. Have group members move around the circle to the right (so they'll hear clearly what is prayed for them without thinking about what they need to pray). Anyone wishing to pray silently may do so, saying, "I'm praying silently." When they're finished, they can say, "Amen."

4. CONTEMPLATING THE SCRIPTURE (*Contemplatio*)

Optional—Read the passage aloud again.

Take a few minutes to sit in silence and enjoy God's presence. If you wish, ask, "God, what is it you most want to say to me at this time?"

Instructions for group leader for *contemplatio:* If you wish, have the passage read aloud again. Read the previous instructions and enjoy a time of contemplation. Close in prayer, thanking God for speaking to members of the group.

HAVING THE HEART OF CHRIST

See also:

- *1 Corinthians 13:4-8, exploring what it means to love (chapter 1)*
- *Luke 8:26-39, Jesus' heart of love and courage for Legion (chapter 7)*

Loving Enemies: Matthew 5:43-48

QUIETING YOURSELF

Center yourself by breathing in and out several times. Surrender each distraction as needed. Be still, and know that God is God.

Optional warm-up prayer—If you're having trouble settling down, offer this prayer:

> *Lord, make me an instrument of your peace.*
> *Where there is hatred, let me sow love.*
> *Where there is injury, pardon.*
> *Where there is doubt, faith.*
> *Where there is despair, hope.*
> *Where there is darkness, light.*
> *Where there is sadness, joy.*
>
> *O Divine Master, grant that I may not so much seek to be consoled*
> *as to console,*
> *not so much to be understood as to understand,*
> *not so much to be loved, as to love;*
> *for it is in giving that we receive,*
> *it is in pardoning that we are pardoned,*
> *it is in dying, that we awake to eternal life.*[4]

Instructions for group leader for Quieting Yourself: If you wish, read the previous prayer aloud. Let group members reflect quietly for a few minutes and then ask them to say aloud the word or words from the prayer that resonate most within them. (If you wish, read it again.)

1. Reading the Scripture *(Lectio)*

Ask the Holy Spirit to speak to you through the words of the following Bible passage, and then read it aloud.

Instructions for group leader for *lectio*: Follow the previous instructions, suggesting that group members close their eyes and listen as you read the Scripture.

A Radical Command

[Jesus said,] "You have heard that it was said, 'Love your neighbor and hate your enemy.' But I tell you: Love your enemies and pray for those who persecute you, that you may be sons of your Father in heaven. He causes his sun to rise on the evil and the good, and sends rain on the righteous and the unrighteous. If you love those who love you, what reward will you get? Are not even the tax collectors doing that? And if you greet only your brothers, what are you doing more than others? Do not even pagans do that? Be perfect, therefore, as your heavenly Father is perfect."

Study Options

If you need to study this passage to understand it better, look at the following italicized words and phrases.

love—Love involves respecting people, being kind to them, and meeting their needs as you are able. This doesn't require affection, but it does help to have a heart for people.

enemies—Listeners probably identified their enemies as their Roman oppressors, but an enemy can be anyone we avoid or find annoying, or who treats us disrespectfully.

perfect—The original Greek word implies completion and maturity. Love completes the law, which is why Jesus said that the Law and the Prophets hang on these two commandments: to love God and love your neighbor (see Matthew 22:37-40). These are a mature expression of the law. The parallel passage in Luke reads: "Be merciful, just as your Father is merciful" (6:36). These parallel verses use different Greek words and are translated differently. Yet this idea that to be merciful is to be mature (perfect) was a life message for Jesus, and he probably preached it in many different ways at many different times.

Instructions for group leader for Study Options: Wait a few minutes after reading the passage, then suggest participants silently read Study Options.

Pondering Options

Use one or both of the following questions to prod your thinking.

1. If you were to pray for an enemy, which of these prayers might you be willing to pray?

> • *Show me the heart of this person.*
> • *What does this person need from me?*
> • *What does this person need from you, O God?*
> • *Is there anything I can do to reconcile with this person?*

2. Here are a few examples of how Jesus showed love to his enemies.

Jesus and His Enemies	How Jesus Showed Love
During Jesus' arrest, a disciple struck the servant of the high priest, cutting off his right ear. Jesus healed it (Luke 22:50-52).	restored the body of an enemy who had been harmed
At the crucifixion, Jesus forgave his executioners on the spot, not holding their deeds against them (Luke 23:34).	forgave enemies and accepted the circumstances as part of God's larger picture
At the request of the legion of demons, Jesus put them into swine instead of into the Abyss (Luke 8:26-39).	lightened the consequences of his enemies
Jesus despised the Pharisees' behavior but wept that they, as leaders of Jerusalem, would have to suffer so much when Rome destroyed Jerusalem (Matthew 23:37-39; Luke 19:41-44).	grieved for the consequences his enemies would suffer

Which of the examples in the column on the left fascinate you most? Which of the actions in the column on the right would you most like to be able to do?

Instructions for group leader for Pondering Options: After the passage is read, ask group members to read silently the previous material, journaling if they wish. After a few minutes, have them choose a pondering option and share their response in a sentence or two.

Cues for Picturing the Passage

Before reading the passage again, consider this cue.

Scenes to picture—To picture an enemy as this passage is read, choose one of these images to represent the enemy:

- *Take the view of the Jews: picture the Romans or Samaritans or any foreign nation.*
- *Take the view of the disciples: picture the Pharisees.*
- *Take a personal view and use the face of someone whom you find difficult.*

When the passage is read again, picture yourself as one of the radically different "children of your Father in heaven" (Matthew 5:45, NRSV).

Instructions for group leader for Cues for Picturing the Passage: Have members read the cue silently. When they're finished reading, continue.

---

2. MEDITATING ON THE SCRIPTURE *(Meditatio)*

Reflect on how your life is touched by this passage today. Read the passage aloud again and ponder this question for several minutes: *What word or phrase or idea emerges from the passage and stays with you?* Reflect a while longer, and consider if God is offering you an invitation in this passage to enlarge your understanding or to do something in the next few days. What might that be? Sit quietly for a few minutes, pondering this question: *What do I need to know from this passage?*

> **Instructions to group leader for *meditatio:*** Have a different group member read the passage aloud and then state the first question in italics above. Have the group sit together quietly for three minutes or more and then ask group members to say the word or phrase or scene that resonates for them. Remind them that they may pass if they wish.
>
> Wait for five minutes or so and ask the second question in italics. Ask group members to respond by saying, "I sense this passage calling me to . . ." and then completing that statement with a short phrase.

3. PRAYING THE SCRIPTURE *(Oratio)*

Read the passage aloud again. Pray, perhaps using one of these suggestions:

- *Tell God how you feel about what you sensed (or didn't sense).*
- *Tell God what you most want to say at this time: "Show me how . . ." or "Thank you for . . ."*

Instructions for group leader for *oratio:* Have another member of the group read the passage aloud. Invite members to pray silently. After a few minutes, ask group members to pray for the person on their left. Have group members move around the circle to the right (so they'll hear clearly what is prayed for them without thinking about what they need to pray). Anyone wishing to pray silently may do so, saying, "I'm praying silently." When they're finished, they can say, "Amen."

4. CONTEMPLATING THE SCRIPTURE *(Contemplatio)*

Optional—Read the passage aloud again.

Take a few minutes to sit in silence and enjoy God's presence. If you wish, ask God, "What is it you most want to say to me at this time?"

Instructions for group leader for *contemplatio:* If you wish, have the passage read aloud again. Read the previous instructions and enjoy a time of contemplation. Close in prayer, thanking God for speaking to members of the group.

BUILDING RELATIONSHIPS

See also:

- *1 Corinthians 12:18-25, needing others and letting myself be needed (chapter 6)*
- *Luke 6:37-43, choosing not to judge others (chapter 6)*

Jesus Serves the Disciples: John 13:1-7,12-15

QUIETING YOURSELF

Center yourself by breathing in and out several times. Bend your neck back and forth and let your muscles relax. Offer each interrupting thought to God.

Optional warm-up exercise—Squat or sit on the floor, facing your empty chair. Get down on your hands and knees as if you were scrubbing someone's floor. Then look up at the empty chair and ponder what it would be like to carry on a conversation with a person sitting in that chair. It is his or her floor you are scrubbing. What would it be like to look up continually to that person and care for that floor?

Then move back to your normal place of meditation, close your eyes and consider, Whose floor would you be willing to scrub, especially if that person were standing over you? Whose floor would it be difficult to scrub?

Instructions for group leader for Quieting Yourself: Read the previous centering instructions and let group members reflect quietly for a few minutes. Once they're back in their chairs, ask if anyone would like to share their thoughts in a sentence or two (keeping eyes closed and speaking slowly).

---

1. READING THE SCRIPTURE (*Lectio*)

Ask the Holy Spirit to speak to you through the words of the following Bible passage, and then read it aloud. If the story is familiar to you, set aside what you know about it and read each word with fresh eyes.

Instructions for group leader for *lectio:* Follow the previous instructions, suggesting that group members close their eyes and listen as you read the Scripture aloud.

THE SETTING

It was just before the Passover Feast. Jesus knew that the time had come for him to leave this world and go to the Father. Having loved his own who were in the world, he now showed them the full extent of his love.

The evening meal was being served, and the devil had already prompted Judas Iscariot, son of Simon, to betray Jesus. Jesus knew that the Father had put all things under his power, and that he had come from God and was returning to God.

THE EXAMPLE

[So] he got up from the meal, took off his outer clothing, and wrapped a towel around his waist. After that, he poured water into a basin and began to wash his disciples' feet, drying them with the towel that was wrapped around him.

He came to Simon Peter, who said to him, "Lord, are you going to wash my feet?"

Jesus replied, "You do not realize now what I am doing, but later you will understand."

THE TEACHING

When he had finished washing their feet, he put on his clothes and returned to his place. "Do you understand what I have done for you?" he asked them. "You call me 'Teacher' and 'Lord,' and rightly so, for that is what I am. Now that I, your Lord and Teacher, have washed your feet, you also should wash one another's feet. I have set you an example that you should do as I have done for you.

Study Options

If you need to study this passage to understand it better, look at the following italicized words and phrases.

leave this world—The events in John 12–19 describe the final week of Jesus' life before his crucifixion.

full extent of his love—Before their deaths, people often want to express the full extent of their love to those closest to them.

wash his disciples' feet—Feet were the primary means of transportation in biblical times and they got dirty and injured because people wore sandals most of the time. Consider how well we would wash the tires of our cars if they customarily rolled into the living areas of our homes and rested under the covers in our beds.

He came to Simon Peter—Imagine Peter watching Jesus move around the group washing feet and finally coming to him. How could their leader do this degrading task? William Barclay wrote, "The disciples of the Rabbis were supposed to render their masters personal service, but a service like this would never have been dreamed of."[5]

Instructions for group leader for Study Options: Wait a few minutes after reading the passage, then suggest participants silently read Study Options.

Pondering Options

Use one or two of the following questions to prod your thinking about this passage.

1. Jesus' unassuming assistance becomes especially meaningful in light of Judas and his plans to betray Jesus.

   - *Jesus was not in safe territory; the enemy's forces were present.*
   - *Jesus served this false friend, who planned to betray him, the same way he served his true friends.*

   Can you think of a time when you served an enemy? If so, when? What was it like?

2. Jesus showed physical signs of vulnerability by

   - *sitting at other people's feet*
   - *taking off outer clothes*
   - *doing the work of a slave*

   The closest thing to a reason Jesus offered for his vulnerability was that he "knew that the Father had put all things under his power, and that he had come from God and was returning to God." Jesus knew who he was. How does that help us with humility?

3. The problem with vulnerability is that it makes us feel as if we have no defense against people who aren't concerned for our best interest. Being vulnerable to others doesn't mean we forget about our own needs but that we present them to God (and sometimes to others) so that together we can figure out how to get those needs met. Sometimes God prompts us to serve people, but we ignore this because we're afraid we won't get our needs met. Consider a time when you were unwilling to help someone. What needs, if any, were you afraid would not get met? Your need to get a word in edgewise? To be respected? To have time to fulfill responsibilities? Your need for rest and leisure? For time alone?

4. How do you respond to Jesus' challenge to attempt such vulnerable service? Is it scary? Threatening, requiring too much risk? Too much work? Beyond your faith? Something you want to try more of?

If any of the previous questions are too difficult, hold them before God for a few minutes and then go on. Don't worry about getting an answer, but be open to what may come to you in the next few days.

Instructions for group leader for Pondering Options: After the passage is read, ask group members to read silently the previous material. After a few minutes, have them choose one pondering option and tell their answer in *one sentence or two*. Explain that this is not a time for discussion, but for reporting responses to the questions.

Cues for Picturing the Passage

Before reading the passage again, consider these cues.

Cultural cue: the inner garment—Men wore an inner garment, usually made of linen or wool, close to the skin. Teachers often wore it down to the feet. This was probably what Jesus wore as he washed their feet. That means he stood there and unwrapped the leather belt and took off his outer garment as well as his *tallith,* a rectangular or square outer garment teachers wore over the top of the body.[6]

Cultural cue: foot-washing—The roads of Palestine were not paved. In dry weather they were inches deep in dust; in wet weather, they were liquid mud. Sandals were nothing more than soles with a few straps. Great water pots were set at the door of most homes, and a servant washed the feet of guests as they came in.[7]

Character cue: Jesus as a leader—Jesus' company of friends had no servants, and no one in this competitive bunch (see Matthew 20:20-28) had taken the role of the servant. Jesus remedied this glaring omission by doing the work no one else would do—foot-washing.

Sense cues: seeing, hearing, touching—If you put yourself in the place of one of the disciples, you can hear the pots being moved and feel the water poured and your feet being rubbed. You would see the Son of God move around the group, washing the feet of people whom you know to be very flawed.

Instructions for group leader for Cues for Picturing the Passage:

Have members read the cues silently. When they're finished reading, continue.

2. MEDITATING ON THE SCRIPTURE *(Meditatio)*

Reflect on how your life is touched by this passage today. Read the passage aloud again and ponder the following question for several minutes: *What word or scene or moment emerges from the passage and stays with you?* Reflect a while longer, and consider: *What is God saying to me today in this passage?*

Instructions for group leader for *meditatio*: Have another group member read the passage aloud and then state the first question in italics. Have the group sit together quietly for three minutes or more and then ask group members to say the word or phrase or scene that resonates for them.

Wait at least five minutes and then ask the second italicized question. Ask group members to respond by saying, "I sense this passage calling me to . . ." and then complete that statement with a short phrase.

---

3. PRAYING THE SCRIPTURE *(Oratio)*

Read the passage aloud again. Pray, perhaps using one of these suggestions:

- *Tell God how you feel about what you sensed (or didn't sense).*
- *Tell God what you most want to say at this time: "Show me how . . ." or "Thank you for . . ."*

Instructions for group leader for *oratio*: Have another member of the group read the passage aloud. Invite members to pray silently, perhaps using the previous prayer suggestions.

After a few minutes, ask group members to pray for the person on their left. Have group members move around the circle to the right (so they'll hear clearly what is prayed for them without thinking about what they need to pray). Anyone wishing to pray silently may do so, saying, "I'm praying silently." When they're finished, they can say, "Amen."

---

4. CONTEMPLATING THE SCRIPTURE (*Contemplatio*)

Optional—Read the passage aloud again.

Take a few minutes to sit in silence and enjoy God's presence. If you wish, ask God, "What is it you most want to say to me at this time?"

Instructions for group leader for *contemplatio*: If you wish, have the passage read aloud again. Read the previous instructions and enjoy a time of contemplation. Close in prayer, thanking God for speaking to members of the group.

MAKING PROGRESS IN THE SPIRITUAL LIFE
See also:

- *Matthew 20:20-28, Jesus' interaction with James, John, and Mama Thunder (chapter 3)*
- *Mark 10:17-22, Jesus' challenging the rich young ruler (chapter 7)*

Choosing the Narrow Door: Luke 13:22-30

QUIETING YOURSELF

Center yourself by breathing in and out several times. Bend your neck back and forth and relax your muscles. Surrender each distraction as needed.

Optional warm-up question—If you're having trouble settling down, consider this question: What progress in the spiritual life has God brought about in you recently? If nothing comes to you, simply enjoy God's presence.

Instructions for group leader for Quieting Yourself: Read the previous centering instructions. After presenting the previous question, let group members reflect quietly for a few minutes. Repeat the question and ask them to share their thoughts in a sentence or two. Anyone who wishes to pass may do so.

---

1. READING THE SCRIPTURE *(Lectio)*

Ask the Holy Spirit to speak to you through the words of the following Bible passage, and then read it aloud.

Instructions for group leader for *lectio:* Follow the previous instructions, suggesting that group members close their eyes and listen as you read the Scripture aloud.

CHALLENGING CIRCUMSTANCES

Then Jesus went through the towns and villages, teaching as he made his way to Jerusalem.

CHALLENGING TALK

Someone asked him, "Lord, are only a few people going to be saved?"

He said to them, "Make every effort to enter through the narrow door, because many, I tell you, will try to enter and will not be able to. Once the owner of the house gets up and closes the door, you will stand outside knocking and pleading, 'Sir, open the door for us.'

"But he will answer, 'I don't know you or where you come from.'

"Then you will say, 'We ate and drank with you, and you taught in our streets.'

"But he will reply, 'I don't know you or where you come from. Away from me, all you evildoers!'

"There will be weeping there, and gnashing of teeth, when you see Abraham, Isaac and Jacob and all the prophets in the kingdom of God, but you yourselves thrown out."

SHOCKING RESULTS

"People will come from east and west and north and south, and will take their places at the feast in the kingdom of God. Indeed there are those who are last who will be first, and first who will be last."

Study Options

If you need to study this passage to understand it better, look at the following italicized words and phrases.

made his way to Jerusalem—Jesus knew that he would die in Jerusalem and had told his disciples so (see Luke 9:43-45,51).

be saved—The accepted answer of the day to this question was that all Jews, except heretics and gross sinners, would enter the kingdom. Jesus refused to speculate and instead spoke directly to the person asking the question.

narrow door—This symbolizes the challenge of the kingdom life—to die to self and live to God. Most people choose the wide gate, but this unpopular narrow door "leads to life" (Matthew 7:14).

east and west and north and south—This largely Jewish audience may have been shocked that the kingdom would include so many nations besides theirs.

those who are last will be first—Popularity, status, wealth, and power are of little value to the kingdom. Knowing Christ is what matters (see Luke 13:25).

Instructions for group leader for Study Options: Wait a few minutes after reading the passage, then suggest participants silently read Study Options.

Pondering Options

Use one or both of the following questions to prod your thinking.

1. In what area of your life has God been challenging you recently to enter by the "narrow door" even if it means being "last" according to someone else's standards?

- *having integrity at work*
- *showing compassion for the throwaways of society*
- *treating people with kindness*
- *wanting to forgive others*
- *other*

2. How shocked would you be if God told you that people far outside your inner circle of comfort would be coming to the heavenly feast?

Instructions for group leader for Pondering Options: After the passage is read, ask group members to read silently the previous material. After a few minutes, have them choose one question and share their answer to that question in a sentence or two.

Cues for Picturing the Passage

Before reading the passage again, consider this cue.

Character cue: People-oriented Jesus—Jesus focused on the questioner instead of the question. Instead of answering the question, "Lord, are only a few people going to be saved?" Jesus addressed the questioner: "[You there, you questioner,] make every effort to enter through the narrow door." What would it look like for you to care deeply about the person who asks questions and to speak to his or her needs instead of trying to come up with a brilliant answer to the questions?

> **Instructions for group leader for Cues for Picturing the Passage:**
> Have members read the cue silently. When they're finished reading, continue.

2. MEDITATING ON THE SCRIPTURE *(Meditatio)*

Reflect on how your life is touched by this passage today. Read the passage aloud again and ponder the following question for several minutes: *What word or phrase emerges from the passage and stays with you?*

Reflect a while longer, and consider if God is offering you an invitation in this passage to enlarge your understanding. What might that be? Sit quietly for a few minutes, pondering this question: *What do I need to know from this passage?*

> **Instructions for group leader for *meditatio:*** Have another group member read the passage aloud and then state the first question printed in italics. Have the group sit together quietly for three minutes or more and then ask group members to say the word or phrase or scene that resonates for them.
>
> Wait for five or more minutes and then ask the second italicized question. Ask group members to respond by saying, "I sense this passage calling me to . . . ," completing that statement with a short phrase.

3. PRAYING THE SCRIPTURE *(Oratio)*

Read the passage aloud again. Pray, perhaps using one of these suggestions:

- *Tell God how you feel about what you sensed (or didn't sense).*
- *Tell God what you most want to say at this time: "Show me how . . ."* *or "Thank you for . . ."*

Instructions for group leader for *oratio:* Have another member of the group read the passage aloud. Invite members to silent prayer, perhaps using the previous prayer suggestions.

After a few minutes, ask group members to pray for the person on their left. Have group members move around the circle to the right (so they'll hear clearly what is prayed for them without thinking about what they need to pray). Anyone wishing to pray silently may do so, saying, "I'm praying silently." When they're finished, they can say, "Amen."

---

4. Contemplating the Scripture (*Contemplatio*)

Optional—Read the passage aloud again.

Take a few minutes to sit in silence and enjoy God's presence. If you wish, ask God, "What is it you most want to say to me at this time?"

Instructions for group leader for *contemplatio:* If you wish, have the passage read aloud again. Read the previous instructions and enjoy a time of contemplation. Close in prayer, thanking God for speaking to members of the group.

Jacob Wrestles with an Angel: Genesis 32:9-12, 24-30

QUIETING YOURSELF

Center yourself by breathing in and out several times. Close your eyes and put yourself in the place of the writer of Psalm 23. You now sit at "a table before me in the presence of my enemies" (verse 5). Those enemies might be hurry, fatigue, or deadlines, but you have these few minutes to sit at a table with Jesus, so disregard those enemies and enjoy the quiet with him.

Optional warm-up question—If you're having trouble settling down, consider this question: *When have you wrestled with God within yourself—or you could have, but didn't?* Close your eyes and take a few minutes to consider quietly your past experiences and the pressing needs in your life. If an answer doesn't come to you at this time, that's fine. Try to enjoy God's presence without having to do anything.

Instructions for group leader for Quieting Yourself: Read the previous centering instructions. After presenting the previous question, let the group reflect quietly for a few minutes. Repeat the question and ask them to share their thoughts briefly in a sentence or two. Anyone who wishes to pass may do so.

---

1. READING THE SCRIPTURE *(Lectio)*

Ask the Holy Spirit to speak to you through the words of the following Bible passage, and then read it aloud. If the story is familiar to you, set aside what you know about it and read each word with fresh eyes.

Instructions for group leader for *lectio:* Pray aloud for the Holy Spirit's leading. Suggest that group members close their eyes and listen as you read the Scripture aloud.

JACOB PRAYS

Then Jacob prayed, "O God of my father Abraham, God of my father Isaac, O LORD, who said to me, 'Go back to your country and your relatives, and I will make you prosper,' I am unworthy of all the kindness and faithfulness you have shown your servant. I had only my staff when I crossed this Jordan, but now I have become two groups. Save me, I pray, from the hand of my brother Esau, for I am afraid he will come and attack me, and also the mothers with their children. But you have said, 'I will surely make you prosper and will make your descendants like the sand of the sea, which cannot be counted.'" . . .

JACOB WRESTLES

So Jacob was left alone, and a man wrestled with him till daybreak. When the man saw that he could not overpower him, he touched the socket of Jacob's hip so that his hip was wrenched as he wrestled with the man. Then the man said, "Let me go, for it is daybreak."

But Jacob replied, "I will not let you go unless you bless me."

The man asked him, "What is your name?"

"Jacob," he answered.

Then the man said, "Your name will no longer be Jacob, but

Israel, because you have struggled with God and with men and have overcome."

Jacob said, "Please tell me your name."

But he replied, "Why do you ask my name?" Then he blessed him there.

So Jacob called the place Peniel, saying, "It is because I saw God face to face, and yet my life was spared."

Study Options

If you need to study this passage to understand it better, look at the following italicized words and phrases.

Save me . . . from the hand of my brother Esau, for I am afraid—Twenty years before, Jacob had gained Esau's birthright from him and cheated him out of his father's intended blessing (see Genesis 25:33; 27:27-40). Esau plotted revenge and so Jacob fled and was now seeing Esau again for the first time.

a man—This man appears to have been a supernatural being. He wrestled for hours without tiring; he dislocated Jacob's hip with a touch; instead of telling Jacob his name, he asked a question to indicate that Jacob should already know his identity; later Jacob considered he had seen the face of God (see Genesis 32:30). Hosea 12:4 refers to the man as an angel.

Your name will no longer be Jacob, but Israel—A name change in the ancient Middle East marked a significant change in the person's life. The name Jacob meant deceiver, but Israel meant "he struggles with God."

Instructions for group leader for Study Options: Wait a few minutes after reading the passage, then suggest participants silently read Study Options.

Pondering Options

Use one or two of the following questions to explore the angelic encounter.

1. When faced with the crisis of meeting his brother, whom he tricked, Jacob chose to ask the angel for a blessing (see Genesis 32:26). Consider a situation you're currently in which is your fault. If an angel appeared to you in the midst of it, what would you ask of that angel?

2. The way God dealt with Jacob is not easy to understand—why wrestle with an angel? God simply spoke conversationally to Abraham and Elijah, but with Jacob he used dreams and wrestling matches to engage him. Jacob was a competitive man, good at outdoing others, "wrestling," so to speak, with people in difficult situations. Suppose an angel appeared to you (although you wouldn't be sure if this person was an angel). How might that angel engage you to get your attention?

   - *meet you on a walk, keep walking with you*
   - *start a conversation with you*
   - *talk with you as a temporary consultant at work*
   - *challenge you to a table game*
   - *ask you to dance*

- *make a surprising comment to you while acting as a clerk at a grocery store*

3. If God were going to give you a new name based on your current progress with God, what might that name be?

	Name Based on Former Character "I used to be a . . . "	Name Based on Current Progress with God "I am now . . . "
Jacob/Israel	"deceiver" (Jacob)	"he struggles with God" (Israel)
Example:	"whiner"	"he cries out to God"
You:		

Instructions for group leader for Pondering Options: Ask participants to read the pondering options silently, choose one, and tell their answer in *one sentence or two.*

Cues for Picturing the Passage

Before reading the passage again, consider these cues.

Character cue: Jacob and his slow progress:

- *Little faith—All his life, Jacob had been good at getting what he wanted from his mother, his father, his brother, even from a difficult person such as his father-in-law Laban (see Genesis 25–31).*

- *More faith*—*While escaping from Esau twenty years earlier, Jacob had experienced a divinely inspired dream of a stairway with angels coming up and down and had been given promises by God. His response*—*a vow*—*indicates that he mustered as much faith as he could: "If God will be with me and will watch over me . . . (here he named many conditions God had to meet) then the* LORD *will be my God." He showed cautious faith*—*"If . . ."*—*and gave God conditions to meet (Genesis 28:1-22).*
- *Mature faith*—*In today's passage, Jacob prayed a contrite prayer full of praise, confession, thankfulness, requests, and references to God's promises. He seemed to realize that nothing would work out without God's input.*

Scenes to picture: riverbank location—Jacob was alone in the grasslands by the bank of the Jabbok River. Foxes, wolves, jackals as well as snakes and scorpions were common, and Jacob, a tent dweller, was outside alone.

Picture Jacob. How do you think he stood? Walked? He was obviously assertive and knew how to make things go his way, a wrestling-match kind of guy. Once you've got him fixed in the picturing part of your brain, read the text again. As you do, picture Jacob

- *praying in fear and distress (see Genesis 32:9-12)*
- *wrestling all night with an angel (see verses 24-25)*
- *pressing the angel for a blessing (see verses 26-29)*

As you read the passage again, picture Jacob alone in the grasslands. Smell the grass and the river. Hear the sounds of the animals at night. Wonder with him, *Who is this strange man approaching?* How does the wrestling match begin?

Instructions for group leader for Cues for Picturing the Passage:
Have members read the cues silently. When they're finished reading, continue.

2. MEDITATING ON THE SCRIPTURE *(Meditatio)*

Reflect on how your life is touched by this passage today. Read the passage aloud again and ponder the following question for several minutes: *What word or phrase, or character, scene, or moment emerges from the passage and stays with you?*

Reflect a while longer, and consider if God is offering you an invitation in this passage to enlarge your understanding or to do something in the next few days. Ponder this question: *What do I need to know from this passage?*

Instructions for group leader for *meditatio:* Have a different group member read the passage aloud and then state the first question printed in italics. Have the group sit together quietly for three minutes or more and then ask group members to say the word or phrase or scene that resonates for them.

Wait for five or more minutes and then ask the second question in italics. Ask group members to respond by saying, "I sense this passage calling me to . . . " and then completing that statement with a short phrase. They may speak with their eyes closed if this helps them remain focused.

3. PRAYING THE SCRIPTURE (Oratio)

Read the passage aloud again. Pray, perhaps using one of these suggestions:

- *Tell God how you feel about what you sensed (or didn't sense).*
- *Tell God what you most want to say at this time: "Show me how . . ." or "Thank you for . . ."*

Instructions for group leader for oratio: Have another member of the group read the passage aloud. Invite members to silent prayer, perhaps using the previous prayer suggestions.

After a few minutes, ask group members to pray for the person on their left, specifically about what the person has sensed from God. Anyone wishing to pray silently may do so, saying, "I'm praying silently." When they're finished, they can say, "Amen."

4. CONTEMPLATING THE SCRIPTURE (Contemplatio)

Optional—Read the passage aloud again.

Take a few minutes to sit in silence and enjoy God's presence. You may wish to use a favorite image. If you wish, ask God, "What is it you most want to say to me at this time?"

Instructions for group leader for *contemplatio*: If you wish, have the passage read aloud again. Read the previous instructions and enjoy a time of contemplation. Close in prayer, thanking God for speaking to the members of the group.

NOTES

CHAPTER 1: WHY MEDITATE?

1. C. S. Lewis, *The Weight of Glory and Other Addresses* (San Francisco: HarperSanFrancisco, 1976), p. 31.

2. Summarized from Douglas Steere, *On Listening to Another,* vol. 2. of *The Doubleday Devotional Classics,* ed. E. Glenn Hinson (Garden City, N.Y.: Doubleday, 1978), pp. 211-214.

3. Norvene Vest, *Gathered in the Word* (Nashville, Tenn.: Upper Room, 1996), p. 11.

4. Another variation is to take the phrase "[speak] the truth in love" (Ephesians 4:15) and substitute the words from 1 Corinthians 13 for "love." So ask God, what would it look like to speak the truth with patience? With kindness? Without rudeness? Without pride? Without keeping a record of wrongs? What if church leaders routinely did such a meditation before any meeting? What would change?

CHAPTER 2: WHY PEOPLE DON'T MEDITATE

1. Psalms 1:2; 19:14; 39:3; 48:9; 77:12; 104:34; 119:15,23,27,48,78,97,99,148; 143:5; 145:5.

2. H. C. Leupold, *Exposition on Psalms* (Grand Rapids, Mich.: Baker, 1969), p. 61.

3. Chester P. Michael and Marie C. Norrisey, *Prayer and Temperament* (Charlottesville, Va.: The Open Door, 1991), p. 46.

4. Michael and Norrisey, p. 46.

5. Norvene Vest, *Gathered in the Word* (Nashville, Tenn.: Upper Room, 1996), p. 100.

6. This method was described in the old Baltimore Catechism. As cited in Michael and Norrisey, p. 34.

7. Frank Whaling, ed., *John and Charles Wesley: Selected Writings* (New York: Paulist Press, 1981), pp. 88-89, as quoted in Vest, p. 108.

8. Dietrich Bonhoeffer, *Life Together* (New York: Harper & Row, 1954), p. 83.

9. Brian McLaren, *A New Kind of Christian* (San Francisco: Jossey-Bass, 2001), p. 17.

10. Jean-Nicholas Grou, *How to Pray* (Cambridge: James Clarke & Co., 1955), p. 18.

11. Interview with Dallas Willard, July 31, 2002, Chatsworth, Calif.

12. Whaling, pp. 88-89, as quoted in Vest, p. 108.

CHAPTER 3: WHAT IS SCRIPTURE MEDITATION?

1. M. Robert Mulholland Jr., *Shaped by the Word* (Nashville, Tenn.: Upper Room, 2000), pp. 55-59.

2. Marjorie Thompson, "Praying with Scripture," *Weavings* 5:3 (May/June 1990), p. 37.

3. A. W. Tozer, *The Pursuit of God* (Camp Hill, Penn.: Christian Publications, 1982), p 82.

4. Dietrich Bonhoeffer, *Life Together* (New York: Harper & Row, 1954), p. 82.

5. Paraphrased from Mulholland, pp. 44-46.

6. Mulholland, p. 19.

CHAPTER 4: INVITING GOD TO SPEAK TO YOU

1. Richard Foster, *Celebration of Discipline* (San Francisco: Harper & Row, 1988), pp. 30-31.

2. Dietrich Bonhoeffer in John Mogabgab, "Meditative Bible Study," *Weavings* 2:2 (March/April 1987), p. 34.

3. William Law, *A Serious Call to a Devout and Holy Life*, as quoted in *The Spiritual Formation Bible* (Grand Rapids, Mich.: Zondervan, 1999), across from p. 671.

4. Jeanne Guyon, *Experiencing the Depths of Jesus Christ* (Beaumont, Tex.: The SeedSowers, 1975), p. 27.

5. Dallas Willard, *Renovation of the Heart* (Colorado Springs, Colo.: NavPress, 2002), p. 17.

CHAPTER 5: HEARING GOD WELL IN MEDITATION

1. "The Practice of Listening: An Interview with Madeleine L'Engle," *Crosspoints,* Summer 1997, p. 3.

2. Interview with Dallas Willard, July 31, 2002, Chatsworth, Calif.

3. Dietrich Bonhoeffer, *Life Together* (New York: Harper & Row, 1954), p. 85, emphasis added.

4. Chester P. Michael and Marie C. Norrisey, *Prayer and Temperament* (Charlottesville, Va.: The Open Door, 1991), p. 35.

5. Bonhoeffer, p. 82.

6. Francis de Sales, *Introduction to the Devout Life* (New York: Doubleday/Image, 1966), p. 81.

7. Thelma Hall, *Too Deep for Words: Rediscovering Lectio Divina* (New York: Paulist Press, 1988), p. 33.

8. Hall, p. 32.

9. Bonhoeffer, pp. 83-84.

CHAPTER 6: TASTING THE WORDS OF SCRIPTURE

1. Norvene Vest, *Gathered in the Word* (Nashville, Tenn.: Upper Room, 1996), p. 11.

2. Francis de Sales, *Introduction to the Devout Life* (New York: Doubleday/Image, 1966), p. 88.

3. Chester P. Michael and Marie C. Norrisey, *Prayer and Temperament* (Charlottesville, Va.: The Open Door, 1991), p. 32.

4. Quoted in Thelma Hall, *Too Deep for Words: Rediscovering Lectio Divina* (New York: Paulist Press, 1988), p. 51.

5. De Sales, p. 81.

6. De Sales, p. 88, emphasis added.

7. De Sales, p. 88.

8. De Sales, p. 90.

9. Quoted in Hall, p. 40.

10. Dietrich Bonhoeffer, *Life Together* (New York: Harper & Row, 1954), p. 83.

11. Henri Nouwen, *Making All Things New* (San Francisco: HarperSanFrancisco, 1981), pp. 84-85.

12. Kristin Henderson and Margery Larrabee, *Spiritual Friendship: Deepening Your Relationship with God Through Intentional Friendship* (Baltimore Yearly Meeting of the Religious Society of Friends, 1998), p. 12.

13. Bonhoeffer, pp. 98-99.

14. Anonymous, "Prayer of an Ageing Woman" in Veronica Zundel, ed., *Eerdmans' Book of Famous Prayers* (Grand Rapids, Mich.: Eerdmans, 1983), p. 53.

15. V. Gilbert Beers, *The Victor Journey Through the Bible* (Wheaton, Ill.: Victor, 1986), p. 250.

16. Alfred Edersheim, *The Life and Times of Jesus the Messiah* (Hendrickson Publishers, 1993), p. 156.

CHAPTER 7: THE SANCTIFIED IMAGINATION

1. Marjorie Thompson, "Praying with Scripture," *Weavings* 5:3 (May/June 1990), p. 39.

2. James W. Fowler, *Stages of Faith: The Psychology of Human Development and the Quest for Meaning* (San Francisco: HarperSanFrancisco, 1981), p. 30, emphasis added.

3. Interview with Dallas Willard, July 31, 2002, Chatsworth, Calif.

4. William Johnston, ed., *The Cloud of Unknowing* (New York: Doubleday/Image, 1973), p. 133.

5. John Mogabgab, editorial, *Weavings* 7:1 (Jan./Feb. 1997), pp. 2-3.

6. Gene Edward Veith, *Reading Between the Lines* (Wheaton, Ill.: Crossway, 1990), p. 31.

7. Oswald Chambers, *My Utmost for His Highest* (Westwood, N.J.: Barbour and Company, 1963), p. 30.

8. Anne Broyles, *Journaling: A Spirit Journey* (Nashville, Tenn.: The Upper Room, 1988), p. 45.

9. Broyles, p. 46.

10. Chester P. Michael and Marie C. Norrisey, *Prayer and Temperament* (Charlottesville, Va.: The Open Door, 1991), p. 50.

11. Alfred Edersheim, *The Life and Times of Jesus the Messiah* (Hendrickson Publishers, 1993), pp. 418-419.

12. J. A. Thompson, *Handbook of Life in Bible Times* (Downers Grove, Ill.: InterVarsity, 1986), p. 105.

CHAPTER 8: OTHER MEDITATIVE APPROACHES

1. Eugene Peterson, *Answering God* (San Francisco: HarperSanFrancisco, 1989), p. 100.

2. Keith Beasley-Topliffe, ed., *The Riches of Simplicity: Selected Writings of Francis & Clare* in *Upper Room Spiritual Classics* (Nashville, Tenn.: Upper Room, 1998), pp. 34-35.

3. C. S. Lewis, *Letters to Malcolm Chiefly on Prayer* (New York: Harcourt Brace and Company, 1964), p. 24.

4. Quoted in Beasley-Topliffe, p. 34.

5. Lewis, p. 25.

6. Quoted in Beasley-Topliffe, pp. 34-35.

7. Lewis, p. 28.

8. Chester P. Michael and Marie C. Norrisey, *Prayer and Temperament* (Charlottesville, Va.: The Open Door, 1991), p. 34.

9. Walter Trobisch, *Martin Luther's Quiet Time* (Downers Grove, Ill.: InterVarsity, 1975), p. 10, emphasis added.

10. Spiritual director and retreat leader Wilkie Au uses this exercise with adaptations from Anne Long, "What Works? Some Experiments in Prayer and Reflection," *Can Spirituality Be Taught: Exploratory Essays* (London: Way Publications), p. 114.

11. Glandion Carney and William Long, *Yearning Minds and Burning Hearts* (Grand Rapids, Mich.: Baker Books, 1997), p. 68.

12. Quoted in E. Glenn Hinson, *Spiritual Preparation for Christian Leadership* (Nashville, Tenn.: Upper Room, 1999), p. 56, emphasis added.

13. Interview with Dallas Willard, July 31, 2002, Chatsworth, Calif.

14. These four questions were provided by Dallas Willard in the class "Spirituality and Ministry," Fuller Theological Seminary, June 10-21, 2002, Mater Dolorosa, Monrovia, Calif.

15. Interview.

16. This powerful idea is taken from Michael and Norrisey, p. 65.

APPENDIX B: MEDITATION EXERCISES

1. D. Guthrie and J. A. Motyer, *The New Bible Commentary* (Grand Rapids, Mich.: Eerdmans, 1991), p. 345.

2. J. A. Thompson, *Handbook of Life in Bible Times* (Downers Grove, Ill.: InterVarsity, 1986), p. 22.

3. W. E. Vine, Merrill F. Unger, William White, *Vine's Expository Dictionary of Biblical Words* (Nashville, Tenn.: Thomas Nelson, 1985), p. 297.

4. Francis of Assisi, as quoted in Veronica Zundel, ed., *Eerdmans' Book of Famous Prayers* (Grand Rapids, Mich.: Eerdmans, 1983), p. 30.

5. William Barclay, *The Daily Bible Study: The Gospel of John,* vol. 2 (Philadelphia: Westminister Press, 1956), p. 160.

6. Alfred Edersheim, *The Life and Times of Jesus the Messiah* (Hendrickson Publishers, 1993), p. 428.

7. Barclay, p. 161.

AUTHOR

Jan Johnson has written thirteen books, including *Enjoying the Presence of God* and *When the Soul Listens*. Those two books along with *Savoring God's Word* form a trilogy on these spiritual disciplines: practicing God's presence; solitude, silence, and contemplative prayer; and Scripture meditation. She also has written more than a thousand magazine articles and truckloads of Bible studies. Articles, selected book chapters, and other resources may be downloaded from her website: www.janjohnson.org

Jan speaks frequently at retreats and conferences, teaching about authentic spirituality and transformation into Christlikeness. Besides holding a degree in Christian education, she is a trained spiritual director. She lives in Simi Valley, California, with her family.

OTHER INSPIRING BOOKS BY JAN JOHNSON.

When the Soul Listens

Feeling too busy to connect with God? Feeling as if you aren't hearing Him speak to you? Find spiritual direction through contemplative living that will lead you to find rest and guidance in God.
1-57683-113-2

Listening to God

With fifty-two topically arranged meditations on real-life themes, this book moves meditation out of the realm of mystics and makes this important spiritual discipline something you'll want to learn.
1-57683-050-0

Enjoying the Presence of God

If you long to enjoy God's companionship but aren't sure where to begin, this book offers practical suggestions for learning to be aware of God's presence in every moment of life.
0-89109-926-3